Block
QUILTS
Buster

I Love Churn Dashes

15 Quilts from an All-Time Favorite Block

Compiled by Karen M. Burns

Martingale®
Create with Confidence

Block-Buster Quilts
I Love Churn Dashes: 15 Quilts from an All-Time Favorite Block
© 2016 by Martingale & Company®

Martingale®
19021 120th Ave. NE, Ste. 102
Bothell, WA 98011-9511 USA
ShopMartingale.com

Printed in China
21 20 19 18 17 16   8 7 6 5 4 3 2 1

Library of Congress Cataloging-in-Publication Data
is available upon request.

ISBN: 978-1-60468-805-4

MISSION STATEMENT

We empower makers who use fabric and yarn
to make life more enjoyable.

CREDITS

PUBLISHER AND
CHIEF VISIONARY OFFICER
Jennifer Erbe Keltner

CONTENT DIRECTOR
Karen Costello Soltys

DESIGN MANAGER
Adrienne Smitke

MANAGING EDITOR
Tina Cook

PRODUCTION MANAGER
Regina Girard

ACQUISITIONS EDITOR
Karen M. Burns

COVER AND
INTERIOR DESIGNER
Connor Chin

TECHNICAL WRITER
Beth Bradley

PHOTOGRAPHER
Brent Kane

TECHNICAL EDITOR
Ellen Pahl

ILLUSTRATOR
Sandy Huffaker

COPY EDITOR
Sheila Chapman Ryan

Contents

Bonus Project Online!
Visit ShopMartingale.com/extras to download
the bonus Short Dash quilt for free!

Introduction

One rule of thumb you can count on for good design is repetition. The repetition of shapes and colors in a room creates visual comfort. The same can be said of quilts and quilt blocks.

The repetition of familiar shapes often gives us comfort. Is it because as quilters, we're confident knowing how the shapes fit together? Or is it the comfort of memory—do we recall seeing those blocks in a quilt long ago? Our reasons for finding contentment in the familiar may vary, but the feelings these familiar shapes evoke when combined are universal.

When it comes to all-time favorite blocks, the Churn Dash appears at the top of many quilters' lists. Sometimes appearing under the pseudonym Monkey Wrench, this boxy block with angled corners has just enough edginess to at once capture our attention and our imagination. Its center can be square or oblong, its corners scant or substantial, its overall size small or jumbo. Depending on color placement, its familiar form can shout "I'm here!" or "Can you find me?" Either way, the Churn Dash beckons us to make another quilt using this beloved block to further ensure its popularity for future generations.

Peruse this carefully curated collection of quilts by 15 top-notch designers, all of whom find comfort in sharing their very best Churn Dash quilt designs.

Jennifer Keltner
Publisher and Chief Visionary Officer

Churn Dash Basics

*T*he Churn Dash block dates back to the early nineteenth century, but it's endured through the decades and remains a favorite go-to block among quilters. It's made from elements— usually half-square-triangle units, rectangles, and a square—placed in a Nine Patch–style grid. The simplicity of the layout makes the Churn Dash block quite versatile. As you can see in the creative and diverse designs throughout this book, the Churn Dash works just as well in traditional quilts as it does in those with a more modern look. Before we delve into all of the fun variations, let's learn how to make a Churn Dash block in its most basic form.

Name Game

The Churn Dash block's name is a clue to its long history. The term comes from the design's resemblance to the staff or pole (referred to as the dash) that's used in a traditional wooden butter churn. While Churn Dash is the most common name for this block, you might also hear it called a Monkey Wrench, Double Wrench, Hole in the Barn Door, or Lincoln's Platform, among others. As is the case with many traditional blocks, different names for the same basic design tend to pop up over time depending on the era or region.

Following are instructions for making a 9" square block (9½" including the seam allowances). The traditional Churn Dash block is made from two contrasting fabrics and is composed of a central square, four pieced strip units, and four half-square-triangle units. The fabric used for the center square is also typically used in the outer strip and triangle sections, as the background of the design (fabric A). The inner triangle and rectangle sections form the Churn Dash motif (fabric B). The following instructions incorporate a common method for making two half-square triangles at a time, but you can find an additional method in "Eight Is Great" on page 8.

1. From fabric A, cut one 3½" x 3½" square, two 4⅜" x 4⅜" squares, and one 2" x 15½" strip. From fabric B, cut two 4⅜" x 4⅜" squares and one 2" x 15½" strip.

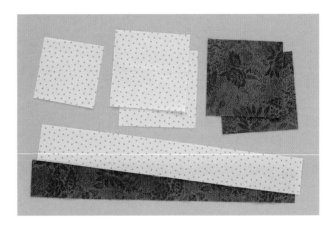

2. Draw a diagonal line from corner to corner on the wrong side of the A 4⅜" squares. Place one marked A square and one B square right sides together. Sew a scant ¼" from each side of the drawn line.

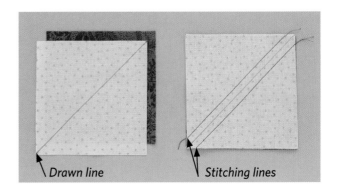

Drawn line   *Stitching lines*

3. Cut along the drawn line to yield two half-square-triangle units. Press the seam allowances toward the darker fabric.

4. Square up and trim the units to measure 3½" square. Repeat with the remaining 4⅜" squares to make a total of four half-square-triangle units.

5. Sew the fabric A and B strips together along one long edge; press the seam allowances toward the darker fabric. Crosscut the strip unit into four segments, 3½" square.

6. Arrange the half-square-triangle units, the strip units, and the fabric A center square in three rows as shown to form the Churn Dash design.

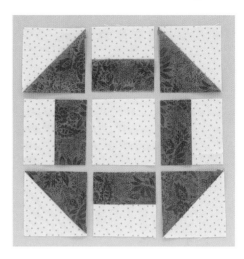

7. Join the units in each row. Press the seam allowances in each row toward the strip units.

8. Join the three rows, and then press the seam allowances toward the middle row.

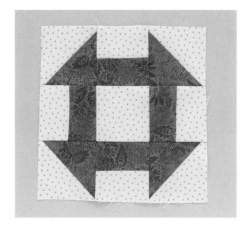

Half-square-triangle units appear in countless quilt blocks and designs. There are many ways of making them, and this method yields eight units at once—which comes in handy if you'll be making lots of Churn Dash blocks.

1. To determine the dimensions of the square you need to cut, add ⅞" to the desired unfinished half-square-triangle size, and then double that number. For a 3½" half-square-triangle unit:

   3½" + ⅞" = 4⅜"
   4⅜" x 2 = 8¾"

   Cut one square, 8¾" x 8¾", each from two contrasting fabrics.

2. On the wrong side of the lighter square, draw perpendicular lines dividing the square in quarters, and then draw diagonal lines from corner to corner in both directions.

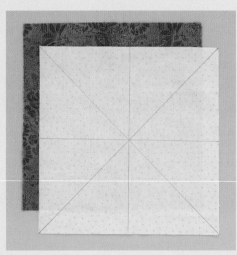

Mark the cutting and sewing lines.

3. Place the squares right sides together. Sew ¼" from each side of both diagonal lines.

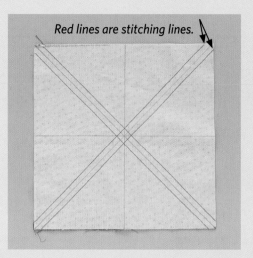

Red lines are stitching lines.

Sew ¼" from each side of both diagonal lines.

4. Cut along *all* of the drawn lines to yield eight half-square-triangle units. Press the seam allowances toward the darker fabric, and then trim and square up each unit to 3½" square.

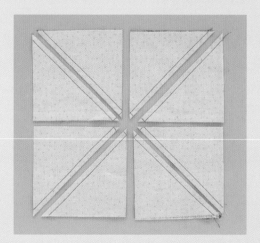

Sew, cut, press, and trim the units.

It's easy to modify the look of the Churn Dash block by altering the size, scale, or color placement of the various units. Check out the following Churn Dash options and be inspired to design your own variations.

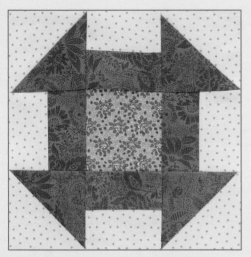

Add a third color to the mix with a contrasting center square.

Make the half-square-triangle units larger than the strip units to create a bolder motif.

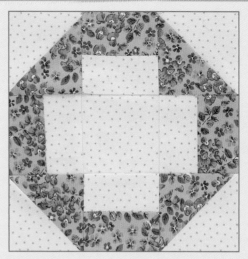

Reverse the color placement of the strip units to create a cross in the block center.

Use a pieced hourglass unit as the center square to add a bit more complexity.

Rotate two of the half-square-triangle units to make an asymmetrical design.

Churn Dash Slide by Christa Watson

Finished quilt: 72½" x 78½" • **Finished blocks:** 12" x 12" and 12" x 6"

Churn Dash Slide

*C*hrista loves to present traditional blocks in new ways. The layout of this quilt, with half blocks at the top and bottom of alternating columns, causes the modern prints in bright colors to slide diagonally across the quilt, giving a new look to an old favorite.

Materials

Yardage is based on 42"-wide fabric. Fat quarters measure approximately 18" x 21" and fat eighths measure approximately 9" x 21".

9 fat quarters of assorted light gray prints for blocks
9 fat quarters of assorted dark gray prints for blocks
12 fat eighths of assorted lime prints for blocks and binding
10 fat eighths of assorted turquoise prints for blocks and binding
10 fat eighths of assorted orange prints for blocks and binding
10 fat eighths of assorted pink prints for blocks and binding
2 fat eighths of different light gray prints for blocks
2 fat eighths of different dark gray prints for blocks
5 yards of fabric for backing
80" x 86" piece of batting

Fabric Notes

If you're purchasing fabric and don't mind a less scrappy look for your quilt, you can make the quilt using 4 fat quarters each of turquoise, orange, lime, and pink prints. Cut the pieces needed for each block from a 5" x 21" strip of fabric.

Don't be overly concerned when using directional prints; let your fabrics flow in any direction for a more interesting look. As you cut, keep like prints together in matching sets.

Cutting

All measurements include ¼"-wide seam allowances.

From *each of 10* assorted lime prints, cut:
    1 strip, 5" x 21"; crosscut into 2 squares, 5" x 5" (20 total)
    Cut the remainder of the strip into 2 strips, 2½" wide; crosscut into
        4 rectangles, 2½" x 4½" (40 total)

From *each of 2* different lime prints, cut:
    1 square, 5" x 5" (2 total)
    2 squares, 2½" x 2½" (4 total)
    1 rectangle, 2½" x 4½" (2 total)

From *each of 8* assorted turquoise prints, cut:
    1 strip, 5" x 21"; crosscut into 2 squares, 5" x 5" (16 total)
    Cut the remainder of the strip into 2 strips, 2½" wide; crosscut into
        4 rectangles, 2½" x 4½" (32 total)

Continued on page 12

Continued from page 11

From *each of 2* different turquoise prints, cut:

    1 square, 5" x 5" (2 total)

    2 squares, 2½" x 2½" (4 total)

    1 rectangle, 2½" x 4½" (2 total)

From *each of 9* assorted orange prints, cut:

    1 strip, 5" x 21", crosscut into 2 squares, 5" x 5"
      (18 total)

    Cut the remainder of the strip into 2 strips, 2½"
      wide; crosscut into 4 rectangles, 2½" x 4½"
      (36 total)

From the *1 remaining* orange print, cut:

    1 square, 5" x 5"

    2 squares, 2½" x 2½"

    1 rectangle, 2½" x 4½"

From *each of 9* assorted pink prints, cut:

    1 strip, 5" x 21"; crosscut into 2 squares, 5" x 5"
      (18 total)

    Cut the remainder of the strip into 2 strips, 2½"
      wide; crosscut into 4 rectangles, 2½" x 4½"
      (36 total)

From the *1 remaining* pink print, cut:

    1 square, 5" x 5"

    2 squares, 2½" x 2½"

    1 rectangle, 2½" x 4½"

From *each* light gray fat quarter, cut:

    1 strip, 5" x 21"; crosscut into 4 squares, 5" x 5"
      (36 total)

    2 strips, 4½" x 21"; crosscut into:

      • 2 squares, 4½" x 4½" (18 total)

      • 8 rectangles, 2½" x 4½" (72 total)

From *each* light gray fat eighth, cut:

    2 squares, 5" x 5" (4 total)

    4 squares, 2½" x 2½" (8 total)

    4 rectangles, 2½" x 4½" (8 total)

From *each* dark gray fat quarter, cut:

    1 strip, 5" x 21"; crosscut into 4 squares, 5" x 5"
      (36 total)

    2 strips, 4½" x 21"; crosscut into:

      • 2 squares, 4½" x 4½" (18 total)

      • 8 rectangles, 2½" x 4½" (72 total)

From *each* dark gray fat eighth, cut:

    1 square, 5" x 5" (2 total)

    2 squares, 2½" x 2½" (4 total)

    2 rectangles, 2½" x 4½" (4 total)

From the remainder of the lime, turquoise, pink, and orange prints, cut *a total of:*

    16 binding strips, 2½" x 21"

Making the Churn Dash Blocks

To reduce bulk, press seam allowances open as shown by the arrows in the illustrations. When pressing seam allowances open, use a slightly shorter stitch length to ensure security. If desired, backstitch at the start and end of each seam to prevent it from coming apart during pressing.

1. Draw a diagonal line from corner to corner on the wrong side of each light and dark gray 5" square.

2. Choose two matching light gray 5" squares and two matching lime 5" squares. With right sides together, layer a light gray square on top of each lime square. Sew ¼" from each side of the marked line. Cut the squares apart on the drawn line and press to make four identical half-square-triangle units. Trim to 4½" square.

Make 4.

Speedy Sewing

Chain piece the units for faster assembly. Pair gray background pieces with the print pieces, stacking the pieces together for each block. Once that's done, you're ready to sew one unit after another without cutting the threads between units.

3. Using the same light gray and lime fabrics and with right sides together, sew a gray 2½" x 4½" rectangle to a lime 2½" x 4½" rectangle along the long edges. Press. Make four.

Make 4.

4. Lay out the four units from step 2, the four units from step 3, and one matching light gray 4½" square as shown. Join the units into three rows and press. Join the rows and press to create the Churn Dash block. The block should measure 12½" square.

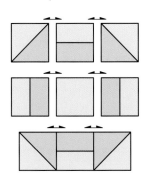 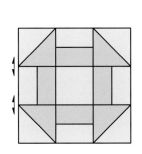

5. Repeat steps 2–4 to make a total of:
   - 10 light gray/lime blocks
   - 8 light gray/turquoise blocks
   - 9 dark gray/pink blocks
   - 9 dark gray/orange blocks

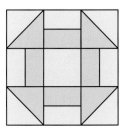 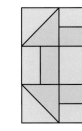

Make 10.   Make 8.

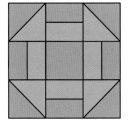 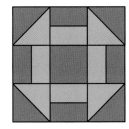

Make 9.   Make 9.

Making the Churn Dash Half Blocks

1. With right sides together, layer a marked light gray 5" square on top of a lime 5" square. Sew ¼" from each side of the marked line. Cut on the drawn line and press to make two identical half-square-triangle units. Trim to 4½" square.

Make 2.

2. Using the same light gray and lime fabrics as in step 1, sew a lime 2½" square to a light gray 2½" square. Press. Make two.

Make 2.

3. Using the same light gray and lime fabrics, sew two light gray 2½" x 4½" rectangles and one lime 2½" x 4½" rectangle together and press as shown. Make one.

Make 1.

4. Lay out the two half-square-triangle units, the two units from step 2, and the unit from step 3 as shown. Sew the units together and press to complete a Churn Dash half block. The half block should measure 12½" x 6½".

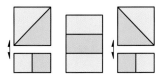

5. Repeat steps 1–4 to make a total of:
   - 2 light gray/lime half blocks
   - 2 light gray/turquoise half blocks
   - 1 dark gray/pink half block
   - 1 dark gray/orange half block

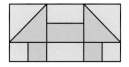

Make 2 of each.

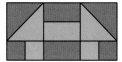

Make 1 of each.

Preserving Points

When joining blocks and rows, use a scant ¼" seam allowance (the width of one or two threads less than a full ¼"). This will ensure that the points on each block will remain nice and sharp.

Assembling the Quilt

1. Referring to the quilt assembly diagram below, lay out the blocks in six vertical rows of one half block and six complete blocks each. Place the half block at the top of rows 1, 3, and 5. Place the half block at the bottom of rows 2, 4, and 6.

2. Sew the blocks in each row together, joining pairs of blocks for faster sewing. Press.

3. Join the rows and press to complete the quilt top. Stitch ⅛" from the edges on all four sides to prevent the edge seams from coming unsewn.

Finishing

Visit ShopMartingale.com/HowtoQuilt for more details on quilting and finishing.

1. Layer the backing, batting, and quilt top; baste the layers together. Hand or machine quilt as desired. Christa chose to free-motion quilt an allover swirl design randomly across the surface of her quilt.

2. Use the 16 assorted 2½" x 21" strips to make the binding and attach it to the quilt.

Quilting Cues

For more creative ways to finish your quilts, check out Christa's books: *Machine Quilting with Style* (Martingale, 2015) and *The Ultimate Guide to Machine Quilting* (with Angela Walters, Martingale, 2016).

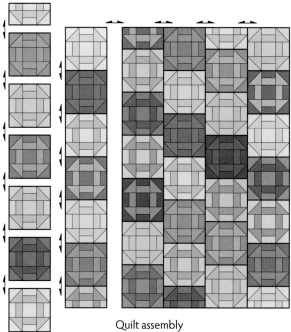

Quilt assembly

Churn Dash Daze

*M*ake an eye-catching Churn Dash design using a spectrum of bold solid colors. The large block is made up of Churn Dashes of varying sizes. The changing scale of the block throughout the quilt makes a lively and dynamic composition.

Materials

Yardage is based on 42"-wide fabric.

7 yards *total* of assorted white and cream solids (lights) for blocks and border

3½ yards *total* of assorted dark solids (teal, navy, raspberry, taupe, and gold) for blocks

⅞ yard of gold solid for binding

7¼ yards of fabric for backing

87" x 105" piece of batting

Cutting

All measurements include ¼"-wide seam allowances. Many of the pieces are of similar sizes. Stay organized by labeling your pieces by size.

From the assorted lights, cut:*

20 strips, 3½" x 42"; crosscut into:
- 120 squares, 3½" x 3½"
- 20 rectangles, 3½" x 6½"
- 20 rectangles, 3½" x 9½"

8 strips, 4" x 42"; crosscut into 80 squares, 4" x 4"

25 strips, 2" x 42"; crosscut into:
- 200 squares, 2" x 2"
- 160 rectangles, 2" x 3½"

4 strips, 3" x 42"; crosscut into 40 squares, 3" x 3"

14 strips, 1½" x 42"; crosscut into:
- 100 squares, 1½" x 1½"
- 400 rectangles, 1" x 1½"

5 strips, 2½" x 42"; crosscut into:
- 20 squares, 2½" x 2½"
- 80 rectangles, 1½" x 2½"

9 strips, 3½" x 42"**

From the assorted darks, cut:

40 *matching sets* of 2 squares, 4" x 4", and 4 rectangles, 2" x 3½"

20 *matching sets* of 2 squares, 3" x 3", and 4 rectangles, 1½" x 2½"

100 *matching sets* of 2 squares, 2" x 2", and 4 rectangles, 1" x 1½"

From the gold solid, cut:

10 strips, 2½" x 42"

*If you're cutting from scraps and don't have enough fabric to cut 42" strips, simply cut the pieces listed for crosscutting.

**You'll need a total length of approximately 360"; strips can be shorter than 42" if you're cutting from scraps.

Churn Dash Daze by Amy Ellis

Finished quilt: 78½" x 96½" • **Finished blocks:** 18" x 18"

Assembling the Blocks

The large 18" blocks are made up of two 9" units, one 6" unit, and five 3" units. Amy's instructions are written for chain piecing all the like units at the same time, regardless of their size. You'll work on all of the blocks at once and each block will be in the same production stage at the same time. You'll be amazed at how quickly they'll come together using this assembly-line method. Keep like colors together as you sew.

Press all seam allowances as shown by the arrows in the illustrations.

1. Draw a diagonal line from corner to corner on the wrong side of the light 4", 3", and 2" squares.

2. Pair each marked square right sides together with a same-size dark square. Sew ¼" from each side of the marked line. Cut on the marked lines, but don't open or press yet.

3. Before pressing, trim the half-square-triangle units to size using one corner of your ruler. Line up the stitching with the 3½" marks for the largest units, and then 2½" and 1½" for the smaller units. Press. Make 160 of the 3½" units, 80 of the 2½" units, and 400 of the 1½" units.

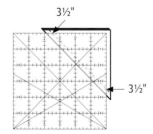

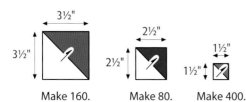

Make 160. Make 80. Make 400.

4. Sew together one dark and one light 2" x 3½" rectangle along one long edge and press. Repeat with all of the remaining rectangles to make 160. Sew the sets of 1½" x 2½" rectangles together in the same manner to make 80 and the sets of 1" x 1½" rectangles to make 400.

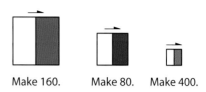

Make 160. Make 80. Make 400.

5. Lay out four matching 3½" half-square-triangle units, four matching 3½" rectangle units, and a light 3½" center square to make the largest churn-dash unit. Sew the units into rows and press. Pin and sew the rows together and press to complete the block. Make 40 of the large 9½" units. Use the 2½" units and a white 2½" center square for the 6½" units; make 20. Use the 1½" units and a white 1½" center square for the 3½" units; make 100.

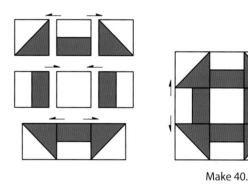

Make 40.

Make 20. Make 100.

6. Pin and sew five 3½" churn-dash units together with four white 3½" squares to make the nine-patch unit as shown. Press. Make 20.

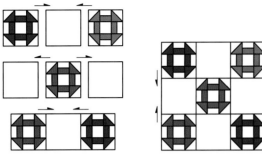

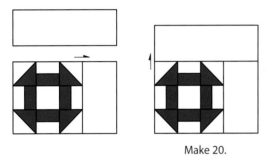

Make 20.

7. Pin and sew a white 3½" x 6½" rectangle to a 6½" unit. Press. Make 20. Sew the light 3½" x 9½" rectangles to the top of the unit and press. Make 20.

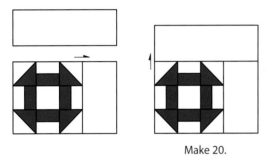

Make 20.

8. Arrange two churn-dash 9½" units, one nine-patch unit from step 6, and one unit from step 7 as shown. Sew the units together in rows and press. Sew the rows together and press to make an 18½" block. Make 20 blocks.

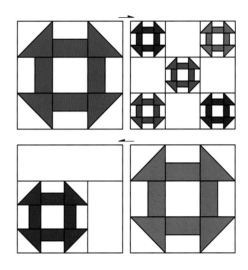

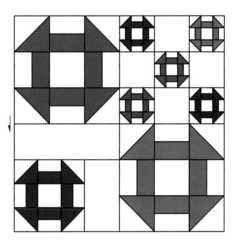

Make 20.

Assembling the Quilt Top

1. Lay out five rows of four blocks each as shown on page 19. Pin and sew the blocks together in rows, then press.

2. Pin and sew the rows together to complete the quilt top. Press.

3. Sew the light 3½"-wide border strips together end to end using a diagonal seam. Trim the seam allowances to ¼" and press.

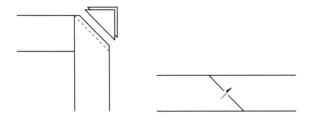

4. Measure the length of the quilt top through the center; it should measure 90½". Cut two strips to this length and sew them to the sides of the quilt. Press. Measure the width of the quilt through the center, including the side borders. It should measure 78½". Cut two strips to this length and sew them to the top and bottom to complete the quilt. Press.

Finishing

Visit ShopMartingale.com/HowtoQuilt for more details on quilting and finishing.

1. Layer the backing, batting, and quilt top; baste the layers together. Hand or machine quilt as desired. Amy quilted a loop design from edge to edge across the surface of her quilt.

2. Use the gold 2½"-wide strips to make the binding and attach it to the quilt.

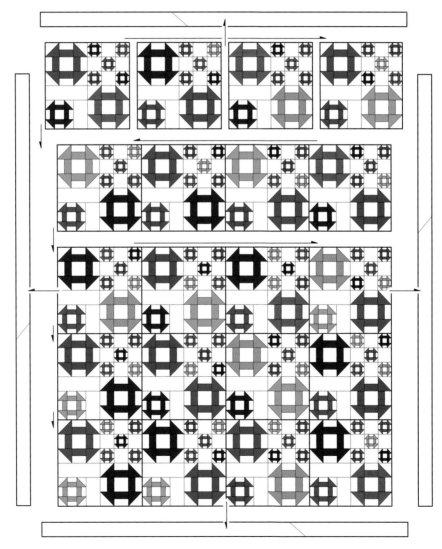

Quilt assembly

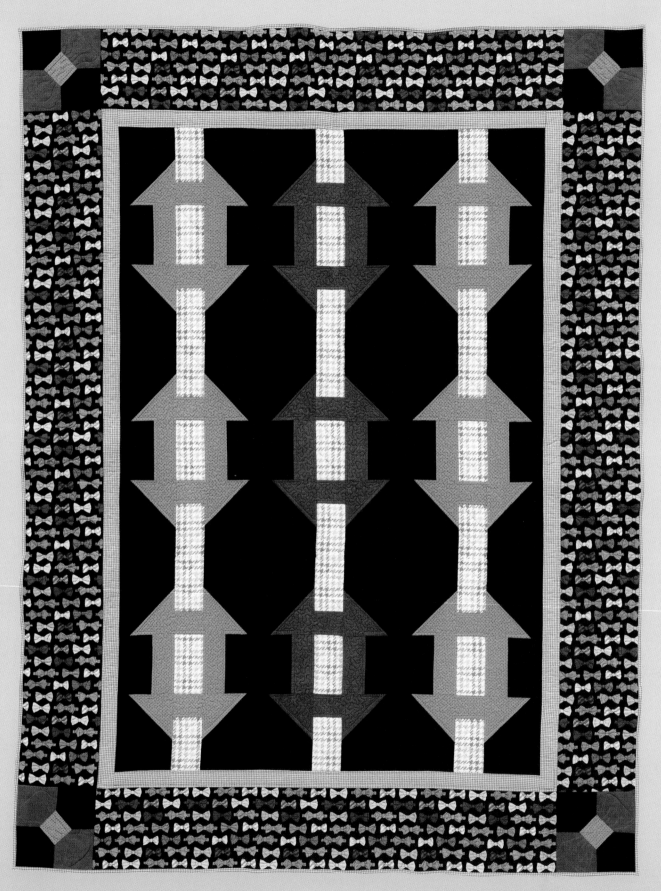

Long Dash by Kari M. Carr; quilted by Penny Miller

Finished quilt: 55" x 71½" • **Finished blocks:** 12½" x 18"

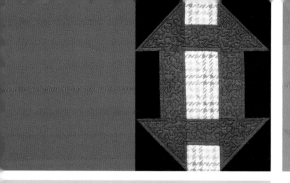

Long Dash

An elongated Churn Dash block brings to mind a playful bow-tie shape, especially when combined with dapper houndstooth and menswear-themed prints.

Materials

Yardage is based on 42"-wide fabric.

2⅛ yards of multicolored print for outer border*

1¾ yards of black tone on tone for blocks

⅝ yard of red tone on tone for blocks

⅞ yard of light gray check for inner border and binding

¾ yard of gold print for blocks

½ yard of gray houndstooth for blocks

3½ yards of fabric for backing

63" x 80" piece of batting

Clearly Perfect Angles tool (optional)

If you choose a print that isn't directional, 1¾ yards will be enough.

Cuddly Option

Kari used plush Minky fabric for the backing of her quilt and omitted batting. If you want to use Minky, you'll need 2⅛ yards of the 60"-wide fabric.

Cutting

All measurements include ¼"-wide seam allowances.

From the black tone on tone, cut:

    6 strips, 7" x 42"; crosscut into 36 rectangles, 5½" x 7"

    3 strips, 3½" x 42"

    1 strip, 4" x 42"; crosscut into 8 squares, 4" x 4"

From the gold print, cut:

    3 strips, 4½" x 42"; crosscut into 24 squares, 4½" x 4½"

    3 strips, 2½" x 42"

    1 strip, 2" x 42"; crosscut into 16 squares, 2" x 2"

From the red tone on tone, cut:

    2 strips, 4½" x 42"; crosscut into 12 squares, 4½" x 4½"

    2 strips, 2½" x 42"

    1 strip, 4" x 42"; crosscut into 8 squares, 4" x 4"

From the gray houndstooth, cut:

    1 strip, 5½" x 42"; crosscut into 9 rectangles, 3" x 5½"

    2 strips, 5" x 42"

Continued on page 22

Continued from page 21

From the light gray check, cut:

5 strips, 2" x 42"; crosscut *2 of the strips* into
    2 strips, 2" x 38"

7 binding strips, 2½" x 42"

From the multicolored print, cut:

2 strips, 7½" x 57½", *on the lengthwise grain**

2 strips, 7½" x 41", *on the crosswise grain**

*If your border fabric is not a directional print, cut all strips on the lengthwise grain.

Making the Block Corners

The instructions are written for piecing by drawing lines on fabric squares. If you're using Kari's Clearly Perfect Angles tool, you don't need to draw any sewing lines; refer instead to the instructions in parentheses. When piecing the blocks using Kari's instructions, you'll make bonus half-square-triangle units at the same time. Use them for another project, or make a small table topper using free downloadable instructions at ShopMartingale.com/extras. (See "Bonus Quilt" on page 24.)

Press all seam allowances as shown by the arrows in the illustrations.

1. Draw a diagonal line from corner to corner on the wrong side of the gold 4½" squares. Draw a second line ⅝" away.

2. With right sides together, place a gold 4½" square on one corner of each of 12 black 5½" x 7" rectangles, making sure the second line is toward the outer corner of the rectangle as shown. Stitch along the center marked lines. (If you're using the Clearly Perfect Angles tool, use center alignment A.) Do *not* trim the seam allowances yet.

3. Stitch on the second marked line of the 12 units to create bonus half-square-triangle units; see "Bonus Quilt." (Use the ⅝" seam guide of the Clearly Perfect Angles tool.) Cut between the two stitching lines and press. Set aside the half-square-triangle units.

Make 12.

4. Repeat steps 1–3 to make a total of 12 units with the gold square on the opposite corner and with the diagonal line running in the opposite direction as shown.

Make 12.

5. Repeat steps 1–3 using the red 4½" squares and the remaining black 5½" x 7" rectangles. Make six of each unit and 12 bonus half-square-triangle units.

Make 6 of each.

Chain Piecing

Speed up your sewing by chain piecing both the first seams and the bonus seams. You can leave the bonus pieces chained together until you're ready to use them. They'll be easier to keep track of this way.

Making the Block Sides

1. With right sides together, stitch a black 3½" x 42" strip to the long edge of a gold 2½" x 42" strip to make a strip set. Press. Make two strip sets. Cut the strip sets into 12 segments, 5½" wide.

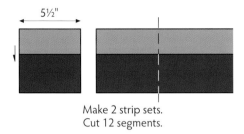

Make 2 strip sets.
Cut 12 segments.

2. Repeat step 1 to sew a black 3½" x 42" strip to a red 2½" x 42" strip. Make one strip set and cut six segments, 5½" wide.

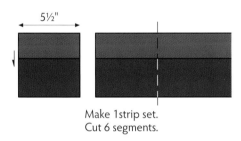

Make 1 strip set.
Cut 6 segments.

3. Sew the remaining gold 2½" x 42" strip to the long edge of a gray houndstooth 5" x 42" strip to make a strip set. Press. Cut the strip set into 12 segments, 3" wide.

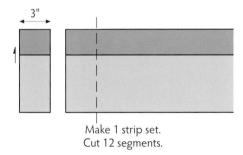

Make 1 strip set.
Cut 12 segments.

4. Repeat step 3 to sew the remaining red 2½" x 42" strip to the remaining gray houndstooth 5" x 42" strip and cut six segments, 3" wide.

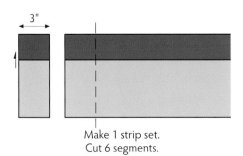

Make 1 strip set.
Cut 6 segments.

Assembling the Blocks

1. Arrange four black/gold corner units, two black/gold side units, two gray/gold side units, and a gray 3" x 5½" rectangle as shown. Sew the units into rows; press. Sew the rows together and press to make the gold Churn Dash block. Make four blocks with the seam allowances pressed as shown and two blocks with the seam allowances pressed in the opposite directions. The blocks should measure 13" x 18½".

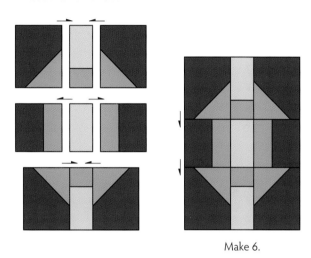

Make 6.

2. Repeat step 1 with the black, red, and gray units to make three red Churn Dash blocks. For two blocks, press the seam allowances as shown in step 1. For the remaining block, press the seam allowances in the opposite direction.

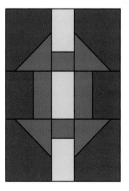

Make 3.

Making the Bow Tie Blocks

1. Draw a diagonal line from corner to corner on the wrong side of the gold 2" squares. (If using the Clearly Perfect Angles tool, you do not need to draw a stitching line.)

2. Place a marked square right sides together on the corner of a black 4" square as shown. Stitch on the drawn line (center alignment A of the Clearly Perfect Angles tool). Trim the corners ¼" from the stitching line and press. Make eight units.

Make 8.

3. Repeat step 2 to sew a marked gold 2" square to one corner of each of the red 4" squares. Make eight units.

Make 8.

4. Arrange two black/gold units and two red/gold units as shown. Sew together in rows and press. Sew the rows together to make the Bow Tie block. Twist the seams at the center and press them in opposite directions. Make four blocks for the border corners. The blocks should measure 7½" square.

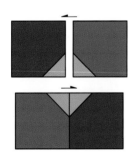 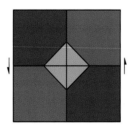

Make 4.

Assembling the Quilt

1. Arrange the Churn Dash blocks in three rows of three blocks each, placing a red block in the center of each row and making sure that the seam allowances will nest when you're sewing the blocks into rows and sewing the rows together. Sew the blocks into rows and press. Join the rows and press.

2. Add the light gray 2" x 38" strips to the top and bottom of the quilt. Press. Join the remaining three light gray strips together end to end to make one long strip. Cut two strips, 57½" long, and sew a strip to each side of the quilt; press.

3. Sew the multicolored 7½" x 57½" borders to each side of the quilt and press.

4. Sew a Bowtie block to each end of the remaining multicolored border pieces, paying attention to the orientation of each corner block. Press.

5. Add the borders to the top and bottom of the quilt and press.

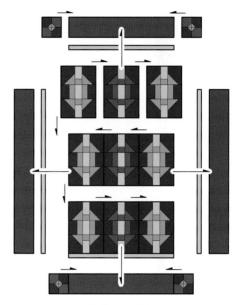

Quilt assembly

Finishing

Visit ShopMartingale.com/HowtoQuilt for more details on quilting and finishing.

1. Layer the backing, batting, and quilt top; baste the layers together. Hand or machine quilt as desired. The quilt shown was quilted in the ditch of the block shapes; the shapes were filled with stippling and pebble designs.

2. Use the light gray 2½"-wide strips to make the binding and attach it to the quilt.

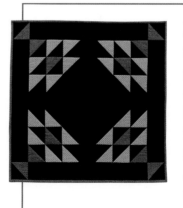

Bonus Quilt

Use your bonus half-square triangles to make this dashing little quilt. Find instructions online at ShopMartingale.com/extras under *I Love Churn Dashes*.

Carriage Wheels

When Carol saw this version of the Churn Dash block in an antique quilt, it reminded her of a wheel with a fancy hub, perhaps like one that might have been found on carriages in the mid-nineteenth century. Combine a variety of prints and colors in a zigzag setting for a scrappy classic.

Materials

Yardage is based on 42"-wide fabric.

2⅛ yards of red floral for outer border and binding

2⅜ yards of gold print for setting triangles

⅓ yard of tan print for inner border

33 scraps, at least 9" x 9", of assorted light prints for block backgrounds

33 scraps, at least 7" x 7", of assorted dark prints (red, brown, blue, and gold) for churn dashes

33 scraps, at least 4" x 4", of assorted dark prints (red, brown, blue, and gold) for nine patches

5 yards of fabric for backing

69" x 88" piece of batting

Cutting

All measurements include ¼"-wide seam allowances.

From *each* of the dark 7" scraps, cut:

2 squares, 3⅛" x 3⅛"; cut in half diagonally to yield 4 triangles (132 total)

4 rectangles, 1¼" x 2¾" (132 total)

From *each* of the light scraps, cut:

2 squares, 3⅛" x 3⅛"; cut in half diagonally to yield 4 triangles (132 total)

8 rectangles, 1¼" x 2¾" (264 total)

4 squares, 1¼" x 1¼" (132 total)

From *each* of the dark 4" scraps, cut:

5 squares, 1¼" x 1¼" (165 total)

From the gold print, cut:

17 squares, 11¼" x 11¼"; cut into quarters diagonally to yield 68 triangles

6 squares, 6" x 6"; cut in half diagonally to yield 12 triangles

From the tan print, cut:

6 strips, 1½" x 42"

From the red floral, cut *on the lengthwise grain:*

4 strips, 6" x 76"

4 binding strips, 2½" x 76"

Carriage Wheels by Carol Hopkins
Finished quilt: 61" x 80" • Finished blocks: 6¾" x 6¾"

Making the Blocks

Each block contains a dark print for the churn dash, a different dark print for the nine-patch center, and a light print for the background. Instructions are written for making one block at a time.

Press all seam allowances as shown by the arrows in the illustrations. For each block, you'll need:

A matching set of:
4 dark 3⅛" triangles
4 dark 1¼" x 2¾" rectangles

A matching set of:
4 light 3⅛" triangles
8 light 1¼" x 2¾" rectangles
4 light 1¼" squares

A matching set of:
5 dark 1¼" squares

1. Sew a dark 3⅛" triangle to a light 3⅛" triangle, right sides together and press. Make four matching half-square-triangle units measuring 2¾" square.

Make 4.

2. Sew a light 1¼" x 2¾" rectangle to opposite sides of a dark 1¼" x 2¾" rectangle and press. Make four matching units measuring 2¾" square.

Make 4.

3. Arrange five 1¼" squares from the second dark print with four light 1¼" squares as shown. Sew the squares together in rows; press. Sew the rows together and press to make a nine-patch unit measuring 2¾" square.

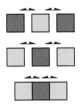

Make 1.

4. Arrange the four half-square-triangle units, four units from step 2, and one nine-patch unit as shown. Sew the pieces together in rows and press. Sew the rows together and press to make a block measuring 7¼" square.

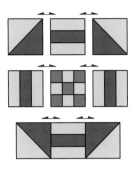 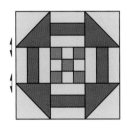

Make 33.

5. Repeat steps 1–4 to make 33 blocks.

Assembling the Quilt

1. Arrange the Churn Dash blocks and gold triangles in five vertical columns. Columns 1, 3, and 5 have seven Churn Dash blocks, twelve large gold setting triangles, and four small gold corner triangles in each. Columns 2 and 4 have six Churn Dash blocks and sixteen large gold triangles.

2. For columns 1, 3, and 5, sew the blocks and the side triangles together into diagonal rows, being sure to keep the long edges of the triangles on the outer edge of the row. Press. The setting triangles are cut oversized and will be trimmed later. Sew the diagonal rows together and press. Add the corner triangles last.

3. For columns 2 and 4, sew the blocks and side triangles into diagonal rows. Press. Sew the diagonal rows together and press.

Rows 2 and 4

Rows 1, 3, and 5

4. Trim and square up the columns to 10" x 67" including seam allowances. Make sure to leave ¼" beyond the points of the blocks for seam allowances.

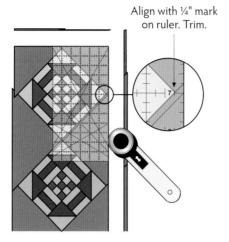

Align with ¼" mark on ruler. Trim.

5. Sew the columns together. The quilt center should be 48" x 67".

6. Sew the six tan 1½" x 42" strips together end to end to make one long strip. Measure the length of the quilt top through the center and cut two tan 1½"-wide strips to this measurement, which should be 67". Sew the strips to the sides of the quilt. Press.

7. Measure the width of the quilt top through the center, including the borders just added. It should be 50" wide. Cut two tan 1½"-wide strips to that length. Sew the strips to the top and bottom of the quilt. Press.

8. Repeat the measuring process to cut and then sew the floral 6"-wide strips to the quilt. The side borders should be 69" long and the top and bottom borders should be 61" long. Press.

Finishing

Visit ShopMartingale.com/HowtoQuilt for more details on quilting and finishing.

1. Layer the backing, batting, and quilt top; baste the layers together. Hand or machine quilt as desired. Carol's quilt features a variety of custom-designed feather and bloom quilting motifs.

2. Use the floral 2½"-wide strips to make the binding and attach it to the quilt.

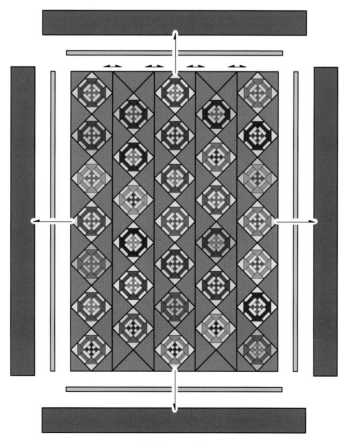

Quilt assembly

Toast and Cheddar by Kim Diehl; quilted by Karen Brown

Finished quilt: 26½" x 26½" • **Finished blocks:** 6" x 6" and 3" x 3"

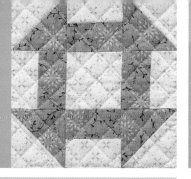

Toast and Cheddar

*C*reate a simply charming Churn Dash quilt in a warm and cozy color combination of cream and cheddar. Frame the alternating blocks with gracefully arched appliqué vines accented by pearly buttons.

Materials

Yardage is based on 42"-wide fabric.

1⅛ yards of cheddar print for blocks, appliqués, and binding

1 yard of cream print for blocks and appliqués

1 yard of fabric for backing

33" x 33" piece of batting

Bias bar to make ¼" stems

Liquid fabric glue (water soluble and acid free)

Freezer paper for placement guide

Supplies for your favorite appliqué method

80 buttons of assorted sizes in shades of cream for berries

Cutting

All measurements include ¼"-wide seam allowances. Cut all pieces across the width of the fabric in the order given. Reserve the remainder of the cheddar and cream prints for cutting the appliqués later.

From the cheddar print, cut:

5 strips, 1" x 42"

1 strip, 2⅞" x 42"; crosscut into:

- 2 squares, 2⅞" x 2⅞"; cut each square in half once diagonally to yield 2 triangles (4 total)
- 4 rectangles, 1½" x 2½"
- 16 squares, 1½" x 1½"

4 strips, 1⅞" x 42"; crosscut into 64 squares, 1⅞" x 1⅞". Cut each square in half once diagonally to yield 2 triangles (128 total).

2 strips, 4½" x 42"; crosscut into 4 rectangles, 4½" x 18½"

3 binding strips, 2½" x 42"

From the cream print, cut:

5 strips, 1" x 42"

1 strip, 2⅞" x 42"; crosscut into:

- 2 squares, 2⅞" x 2⅞"; cut each square in half once diagonally to yield 2 triangles (4 total)
- 4 rectangles, 1½" x 2½"
- 16 squares, 1½" x 1½"

4 strips, 1⅞" x 42"; crosscut into 64 squares, 1⅞" x 1⅞". Cut each square in half once diagonally to yield 2 triangles (128 total).

1 strip, 4½" x 42"; crosscut into:

- 4 squares, 4½" x 4½"
- 1 square, 2½" x 2½"

Making the Large Churn Dash Block

Press all seam allowances as shown by the arrows in the illustrations.

1. Sew a cheddar 2⅞" triangle to a cream 2⅞" triangle along the long diagonal edges; press. Trim the dog-ear points (small triangles that extend beyond the square). Make four half-square-triangle units measuring 2½" square.

Make 4.

2. Sew the cheddar and cream 1½" x 2½" rectangles together along the long edges and press. Make four pieced units measuring 2½" square.

Make 4.

3. Lay out the half-square-triangle units, the pieced units, and the cream 2½" square as shown to form the block. Join the pieces in each horizontal row and press. Join the rows. Press. The large Churn Dash block should measure 6½" square.

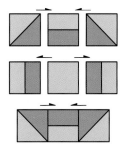 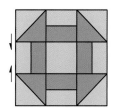

Making the Small Churn Dash Blocks

1. Sew cheddar and cream 1" x 42" strips together along the long edges to make a strip set; press. Make five strip sets measuring 1½" x 42". Cut the strip sets into 1½"-wide segments to make 128 pieced units.

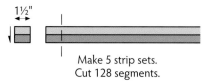

Make 5 strip sets.
Cut 128 segments.

2. Using cheddar and cream 1⅞" triangles, repeat step 1 of "Making the Large Churn Dash Blocks" to piece 128 half-square-triangle units measuring 1½" square.

3. Lay out and sew four half-square-triangle units, four pieced units, and a cream 1½" square as you did for the large Churn Dash blocks to make a block measuring 3½" square. Make a total of 16 blocks with cream centers.

Make 16.

4. Repeat step 3, substituting a cheddar 1½" square for the center square and reversing the position of the cream and cheddar prints. Press the seam allowances in opposite directions from the blocks made in step 3. Make 16 blocks with cheddar centers.

Make 16.

Assembling the Quilt Center

1. Lay out three small Churn Dash blocks with cream centers and three small Churn Dash blocks with cheddar centers as shown. Sew the blocks together in rows; press. Sew the rows together and press to make a corner section measuring 6½" x 9½". Make four corner sections.

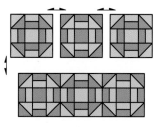

Make 4.

2. Lay out two small blocks with cream centers and two small blocks with cheddar centers as shown. Join the blocks in each horizontal row; press. Join the rows and press to make a side section measuring 6½" square. Make two side sections.

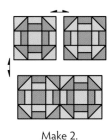

Make 2.

3. Join a side section to the right and left sides of the large Churn Dash block. The center row should measure 6½" x 18½".

4. Lay out the center row and corner sections as shown, making sure the units alternate correctly. Join the corner sections and then join the rows. The quilt center should measure 18½" square.

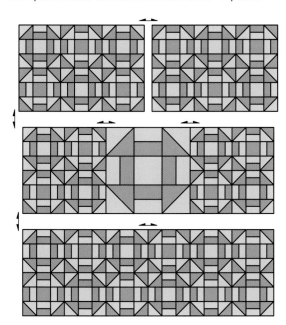

Preparing the Appliqués

Visit ShopMartingale.com/HowtoQuilt for more details on various appliqué methods. Kim used her easy invisible machine-appliqué method for this project. Find details in her book *Simple Appliqué* (Martingale, 2015).

1. Using a rotary cutter and an acrylic ruler, cut eight bias strips measuring 1" x 8" from the reserved cream print.

2. Fold each strip in half with *wrong* sides together and use a *scant* ¼" seam allowance to sew along the long raw edges to make tubes.

3. Insert the bias bar into each tube to press it flat, centering the seam allowance so it will be hidden on the back. Remove the bar and press each stem a second time; trim the seam allowance if needed.

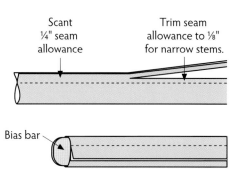

Scant ¼" seam allowance

Trim seam allowance to ⅛" for narrow stems.

Bias bar

4. Apply small dots of liquid fabric glue at ½" to 1" intervals underneath the pressed seam allowances of each stem; use a hot, dry iron to heat set and anchor the seams in place.

5. Apply a small amount of liquid glue (or fabric glue stick, if you prefer) to the wrong side of one raw end of a prepared stem. Turn the end of the stem under approximately ¼" and use a hot, dry iron to heat set the glue and anchor the raw end on the wrong side of the stem. Repeat with the remaining stems.

6. Using your favorite appliqué method and the patterns on page 35, prepare the following appliqués:
   • 40 small leaves from cream print
   • 8 oak leaves from cream print (Kim cut some of the oak leaves reversed.)
   • 16 small leaves from cheddar print

7. With a pencil, trace the stem placement guide on page 35 onto the dull, nonwaxy side of a piece of freezer paper; include the notes and leaf-placement marks. Layer a second piece of freezer paper on the marked paper, waxy sides together. Press with a hot, dry iron to fuse the layers; cut out the shape to make a placement guide for the stem. Add oak-leaf placement marks to the reverse, unmarked side of the freezer paper.

Adding the Appliqués

1. Position the freezer-paper guide on the lower-left corner of a cheddar 4½" x 18½" border strip; pin in place. Dot the seam allowance of a prepared bias stem with liquid glue at approximately ½" to 1" intervals. Beginning at the inside edge of the guide, lay out the prepared stem along the edge of the freezer paper. Allow the excess stem length to extend beyond the left edge of the border.

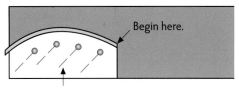

Freezer paper guide

2. With the guide still in place, position a prepared oak leaf on the guide where indicated, tucking the raw end of the leaf underneath the stem; if needed, trim away a bit of the oak-leaf stem so that it's well hidden underneath the bias stem. Remove the freezer-paper guide and pin or baste the oak leaf in place.

3. Flip the guide over so the shape is reversed and repeat the process on the opposite end of the cheddar border strip, placing the marked corner in the bottom-right corner of the border strip.

4. Referring to the quilt photo on page 30 as a guide, position and baste five small cream leaves along each stem.

5. Use your favorite appliqué method to stitch the appliqués in place. Note that the button berries will be added after the quilt has been quilted.

6. Repeat steps 1–5 to appliqué all four cheddar border strips.

Adding the Borders and Completing the Appliqué

1. Sew an appliquéd cheddar border strip to the right and left sides of the quilt center. Press.

2. Sew a cream 4½" square to each end of the remaining appliquéd border strips. Press. Add these strips to the top and bottom of the quilt center. Press. The quilt top should now measure 26½" square.

3. Referring to the quilt photo, position four small cheddar leaves in each cream corner of the border. Pin or baste the bottom leaf first, and then appliqué it in place. Add the second leaf and appliqué it, slightly overlapping the leaf below.

Quilt assembly

Finishing

Visit ShopMartingale.com/HowtoQuilt for more details on quilting and finishing.

1. Layer the backing, batting, and quilt top; baste the layers together. Hand or machine quilt as desired. The featured quilt was machine quilted with a 1" diagonal crosshatching pattern on the center large Churn Dash block. A freeform feathered-swirl pattern was quilted on the small Churn Dash blocks, and the diagonal crosshatching was repeated in the border (with the stitching placed on top of the appliqués).

2. Use the cheddar 2½"-wide strips to make the binding and attach it to the quilt.

3. Using a needle and a double strand of cream thread, stitch the buttons to the quilt top to form berries, burying the knots between the quilt layers. Refer to the quilt photo for placement guidance. For a different look, you can tie a knot at the center of each stitched button and clip the threads to leave decorative tails.

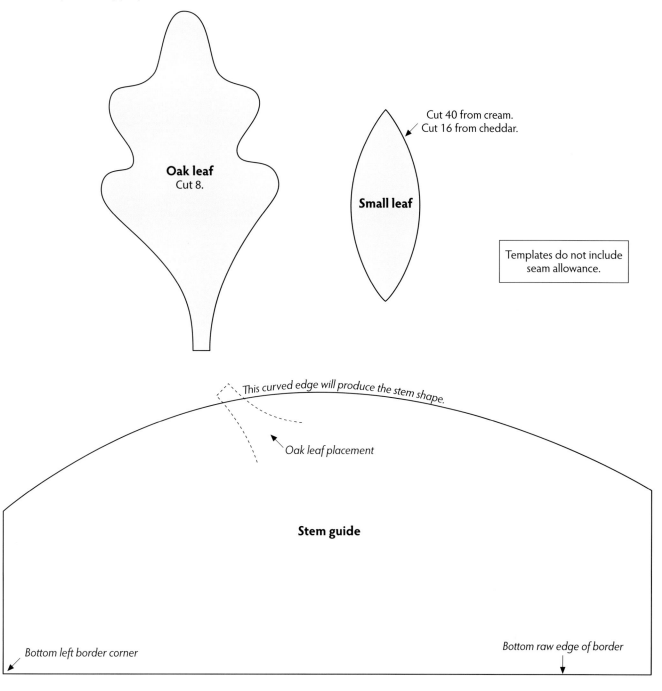

Oak leaf
Cut 8.

Cut 40 from cream.
Cut 16 from cheddar.

Small leaf

Templates do not include seam allowance.

This curved edge will produce the stem shape.

Oak leaf placement

Stem guide

Bottom left border corner

Bottom raw edge of border

In Reverse by Kate Henderson
Quilt 1: Patchwork Churn Dash
Finished quilt: 36½" x 36½"

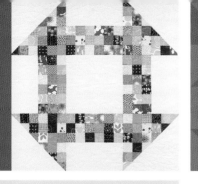

In Reverse

*T*wo quilts are better than one! Play with positive and negative space to make a pair of supersized Churn Dash designs. The patchwork squares are all 2½", an ideal size for using up fabric scraps and leftovers from precut strips and squares. If you want to make both the quilt shown on page 36 and the one on page 39, refer to "Making Both Quilts" on page 40 for combined materials and cutting lists.

Quilt 1: Patchwork Churn Dash

Materials for Patchwork Churn Dash

Yardage is based on 42"-wide fabric.

13 strips, 2½" x 42", of assorted prints for block

⅞ yard of white solid for background

½ yard of red tone on tone for binding

1⅓ yards of fabric for backing

42" x 42" piece of batting

Cutting for Patchwork Churn Dash

All measurements include ¼" seam allowances.

From *each* of the 13 print strips, cut:

  12 squares, 2½" x 2½" (156 total)

From the white solid, cut:

  2 strips, 6½" x 42"; crosscut into 4 rectangles, 6½" x 12½"

  1 strip, 12⅞" x 42"; crosscut into:

    • 2 squares, 12⅞" x 12⅞"; cut in half diagonally to yield 4 triangles

    • 1 square, 12½" x 12½"

From the red tone on tone, cut:

  5 strips, 2½" x 42"

Making the Block Sides

Kate pressed all of the seam allowances open to reduce bulk, but feel free to press them to one side if desired.

1. Arrange 18 print 2½" squares in three rows of six squares each. Sew the squares together in rows and press. Join the rows. Press. Make four.

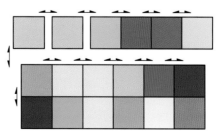

Make 4.

2. Sew a white 6½" x 12½" rectangle to a unit from step 1; press. Make four.

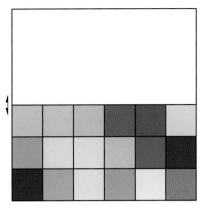

Make 4.

Making the Block Corners

1. Draw a diagonal line from corner to corner on the wrong side of 24 of the print 2½" squares. Trim ¼" from the diagonal as shown. Keep the larger triangles; discard or save the smaller triangles as desired.

Discard.

Trim.

2. Arrange 15 print 2½" squares and six triangles from step 1 as shown. Sew together into rows; press. Sew the rows together and press. Make four.

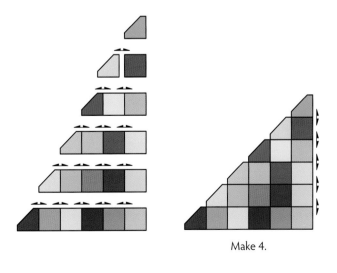

Make 4.

3. Sew a white 12⅞" triangle to a unit from step 2; press. Make four.

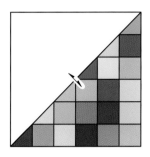

Make 4.

Assembling the Quilt

Arrange four block sides, four block corners, and the white 12½" square in three rows of three as shown. Sew the blocks and square together in rows; press. Sew the rows together and press.

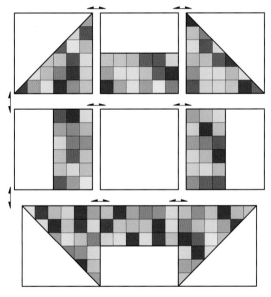

Assembly diagram

Finishing

Visit ShopMartingale.com/HowtoQuilt for more details on quilting and finishing.

1. Layer the backing, batting, and quilt top; baste the layers together. Hand or machine quilt as desired. Kate machine quilted this quilt with a pattern of overlapping triangles.

2. Use the red 2½"-wide strips to make the binding and attach it to the quilt.

Quilt 2:
Solid Churn Dash

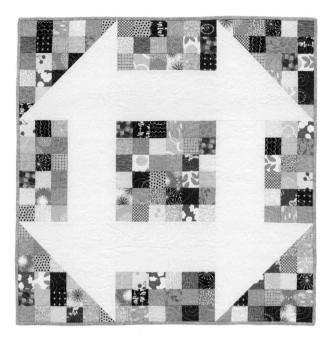

In Reverse by Kate Henderson
Quilt 2: Solid Churn Dash
Finished quilt: 36½" x 36½"

Materials for Solid Churn Dash

Yardage based on 42"-wide fabric.

16 strips, 2½" x 42", of assorted prints for background

⅞ yard of white solid for block

½ yard of gold print for binding

1⅓ yards of fabric for backing

42" x 42" piece of batting

Cutting for Solid Churn Dash

All measurements include ¼"-wide seam allowances.

From *each* of the 16 print strips, cut:

  12 squares, 2½" x 2½" (192 total)

From the white solid, cut:

  2 strips, 6½" x 42"; crosscut into 4 rectangles,
    6½" x 12½"

  1 strip, 12⅞" x 42"; crosscut into 2 squares,
    12⅞" x 12⅞". Cut in half diagonally to yield
    4 triangles.

From the gold print, cut:

  5 strips, 2½" x 42"

Making the Block Sides and Corners

Refer to "Making the Block Sides" on page 37 and "Making the Block Corners" on page 38 for the Patchwork Churn Dash. All steps are the same for the Solid Churn Dash. Kate pressed all of the seam allowances open to reduce bulk, but feel free to press them to one side if desired.

Making the Block Center

Arrange 36 print 2½" squares in six rows of six squares each. Sew the squares together in rows; press. Sew the rows together and press. Make one.

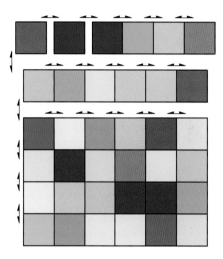

Assembling the Quilt

Arrange four block sides, four block corners, and the block center in three rows of three as shown. Sew the units together in rows; press. Sew the rows together and press.

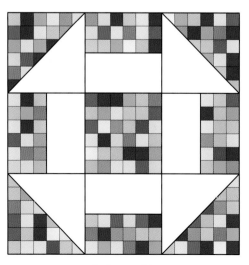

Quilt assembly

Finishing

Visit ShopMartingale.com/HowtoQuilt for more details on quilting and finishing.

1. Layer the backing, batting, and quilt top; baste the layers together. Hand or machine quilt as desired. Kate machine quilted this version with an allover wave design.

2. Use the gold 2½"-wide strips to make the binding and attach it to the quilt.

Making Both Quilts

If you'd like to make both versions of the In Reverse quilt at the same time, use the materials and cutting lists below. Then follow the steps for making each of the quilts beginning on page 37.

Materials for Both Quilts

Yardage based on 42"-wide fabric.

25 strips, 2½" x 42", of assorted prints for blocks and background

1⅜ yards of white fabric for blocks and background

½ yard *each* of red and gold prints for binding (or ⅞ yard *total* if using one fabric for both)

1⅓ yards *each* of two fabrics for backing (or 2⅝ yards *total* if using one fabric for both)

2 pieces of batting, 42" x 42"

Cutting for Both Quilts

All measurements include ¼"-wide seam allowances.

From *each* of the 25 print strips, cut:

14 squares, 2½" x 2½" (350 total; 2 squares are extra)

From the white fabric, cut:

3 strips, 6½" x 42"; crosscut into 8 rectangles, 6½" x 12½"

2 strips, 12⅞" x 42"; crosscut into:
• 4 squares, 12⅞" x 12⅞"; cut in half diagonally to yield 8 triangles
• 1 square, 12½" x 12½"

From *each* binding fabric, cut:

5 strips, 2½" x 42" (10 total)

Block Party

Make cheery Churn Dash blocks using a vibrant palette reminiscent of a summertime celebration. The inclusion of solid white squares in the mix creates a playful, asymmetrical layout.

Materials

Yardage is based on 42"-wide fabric.

2⅞ yards of white solid for blocks and border

¼ yard *each* of orange, pink, green, turquoise, and yellow solids for blocks

⅝ yard of pink solid for binding

3¼ yards of fabric for backing

57" x 75" piece of batting

Cutting

All measurements include ¼"-wide seam allowances.

From the white solid, cut:

5 strips, 3⅞" x 42"; crosscut into 48 squares, 3⅞" x 3⅞"

7 strips, 3½" x 42"; crosscut into:
- 96 rectangles, 2" x 3½"
- 24 squares, 3½" x 3½"

3 strips, 9½" x 42"; crosscut into 11 squares, 9½" x 9½"

6 strips, 2½" x 42"

From *each* of the turquoise, orange, pink, and yellow solids, cut:

1 strip, 3⅞" x 42"; crosscut into 10 squares, 3⅞" x 3⅞" (40 total)

1 strip, 3½" x 42"; crosscut into 20 rectangles, 2" x 3½" (80 total)

From the green solid, cut:

1 strip, 3⅞" x 42"; crosscut into 8 squares, 3⅞" x 3⅞"

1 strip, 3½" x 42"; crosscut into 16 rectangles, 2" x 3½"

From the pink solid for binding, cut:

7 strips, 2½" x 42"

Block Party by Jackie White
Finished quilt: 49½" x 67½" • **Finished blocks:** 9" x 9"

Making the Blocks

Press all seam allowances as shown by the arrows in the illustrations.

1. Using a pencil or your favorite fabric marker, draw a diagonal line from corner to corner on the wrong side of the white 3⅞" squares.

2. Layer a marked white square right sides together with a turquoise 3⅞" square. Sew a scant ¼" from each side of the drawn line. Cut apart on the drawn line and press. Repeat with all of the turquoise squares. You'll have 20 half-square-triangle units measuring 3½" square.

Make 20.

3. Sew a white 2" x 3½" rectangle to a turquoise 2" x 3½" rectangle along the long sides; press. Make 20.

Make 20.

4. Arrange four half-square-triangle units, four rectangle units, and a white 3½" square in three rows as shown. Sew the units into rows; press. Sew the rows together and press. Make five turquoise and white blocks, which should measure 9½" square.

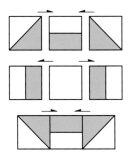 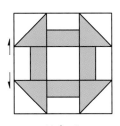

Make 5.

5. Repeat steps 2–4 using the orange, pink, and yellow squares and rectangles to make five blocks of each color. Repeat using the green squares and rectangles to make four green blocks.

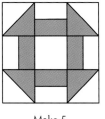

Make 5.   Make 5.

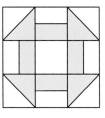 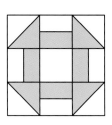

Make 5.   Make 4.

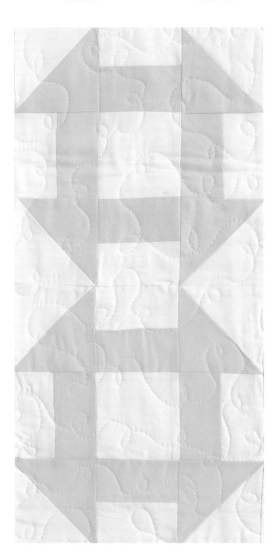

Assembling the Quilt

1. Referring to the assembly diagram below, lay out the blocks and white 9½" squares in seven rows of five each. Sew into rows and press. Sew the rows together and press.

2. Piece the white 2½" x 42" strips together to make one long strip. Cut two strips, 45½" long, for the top and bottom borders. Cut two strips, 67½" long, for the side borders.

3. Sew the shorter strips to the top and bottom of the quilt; press. Sew the longer strips to the sides of the quilt and press.

Finishing

Visit ShopMartingale.com/HowtoQuilt for more details on quilting and finishing.

1. Layer the backing, batting, and quilt top; baste the layers together. Hand or machine quilt as desired. Jackie's quilt was quilted with an allover design of loops and swirls.

2. Use the pink 2½"-wide strips to make the binding and attach it to the quilt.

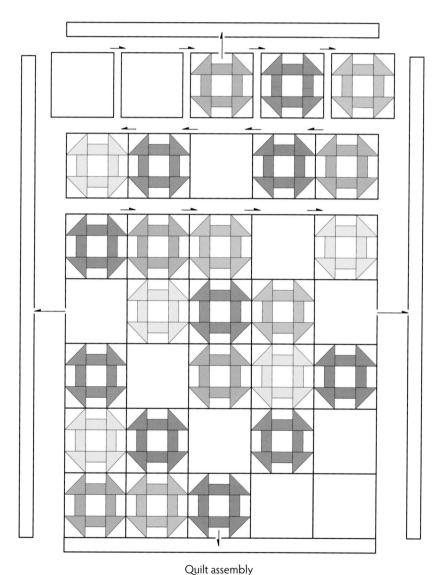

Quilt assembly

Wind Rows

*B*lue, red, and tan combine in this fresh and simple color scheme. The clever addition of triangles at the block corners, combined with sashing squares, gives the illusion of two different-sized blocks and creates a striking diagonal layout in this king-size quilt.

Materials

Yardage is based on 42"-wide fabric.

4 yards *total* of assorted tan prints for blocks

3¾ yards of tan solid for setting triangles and middle border

2⅓ yards *total* of assorted blue prints for blocks

1⅞ yards of blue print for outer border and binding

1¼ yards of red print for blocks, sashing squares, and inner border

8⅔ yards of fabric for backing

104" x 104" piece of batting

Cutting

All measurements include ¼"-wide seam allowances.

From the assorted blue prints, cut:

85 matching sets of:
- 2 squares, 3⅞" x 3⅞"; cut in half diagonally to make 4 triangles (340 total)
- 1 square, 2" x 2" (85 total)

From the assorted tan prints, cut:

85 matching sets of:
- 2 squares, 3⅞" x 3⅞"; cut in half diagonally to make 4 triangles (340 total)
- 4 rectangles, 2" x 3½" (340 total)

From the red print, cut:

26 strips, 1½" x 42"; crosscut *17 of the strips* into 420 squares, 1½" x 1½"

From the tan solid, cut:

7 strips, 8" x 42"; crosscut into 172 rectangles, 1½" x 8"

1 strip, 9" x 42"; crosscut into 20 rectangles, 1½" x 9"

6 squares, 13½" x 13½"; cut into quarters diagonally to make 24 triangles

2 squares, 8" x 8"; cut in half diagonally to make 4 triangles

9 strips, 2" x 42"

From the blue print, cut:

10 strips, 3½" x 42"

10 binding strips, 2½" x 42"

Wind Rows by Laura Boehnke; quilted by Sue Urich

Finished quilt: 95½" x 95½" • **Finished blocks:** 7½" x 7½"

Making the Blocks

Press all seam allowances as shown by the arrows in the illustrations.

1. To make one block, you'll need the following pieces from one blue print and one tan print:
   - 4 matching blue 3⅞" triangles
   - 1 matching blue 2" square
   - 4 matching tan 3⅞" triangles
   - 4 matching tan 2" x 3½" rectangles

2. Sew a blue triangle to a tan triangle along the diagonal edges to make a half-square-triangle unit; press. Make four.

Make 4.

3. Arrange the four half-square-triangle units, four tan 2" x 3½" rectangles, and the blue 2" square into three rows as shown. Sew the pieces together in rows; press. Sew the rows together and press. The block should measure 8" square.

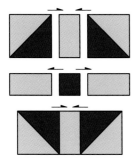 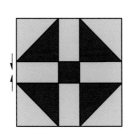

4. Repeat steps 1–3 to make 85 blocks.

5. Draw a diagonal line from corner to corner on the wrong side of 336 red 1½" squares.

6. Place a marked red square on each corner of a block as shown, right sides together. Sew along the marked lines. Press the triangle toward the corner and trim the seam allowances to ¼" to make a center block. Make 61 center blocks.

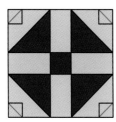 

Make 61.

7. Repeat step 6 with three marked red 1½" squares to make a side block as shown. Make 20 side blocks.

Make 20.

8. Repeat step 6 with two marked red 1½" squares to make a corner block as shown. Make four corner blocks.

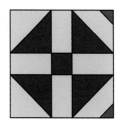

Make 4.

Making the Pieced Side Setting Triangles

Place one of the remaining marked red 1½" squares on the 90° corner of a tan 13½" triangle as shown. Sew along the marked line. Press the red triangle toward the corner and trim the seam allowances to ¼". Repeat to make a total of 24 pieced side triangles.

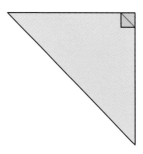 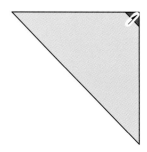

Make 24.

Assembling the Quilt Top

1. Arrange the blocks, sashing pieces, and setting triangles in diagonal rows as shown below, placing the tan 8" sashing strips between the blocks and the 9" sashing strips between the block and setting triangle at each row end. Sew the blocks and sashing together to make 13 block rows; sew the sashing and red squares together to make 12 sashing rows. Press. Do not add the corner triangles yet.

2. Sew the rows together and add the corner triangles to finish the quilt center. Press the seam allowances in one direction.

3. Trim the quilt on all sides so that the quilt center measures 84½" square. This would be ⅝" beyond the block points on all sides if everything is mathematically correct. Measure your quilt through the center in both directions after trimming. If necessary, modify the length of the border strips in the steps that follow to match the quilt dimensions.

Ruler Assistance

A large 20½" square ruler is helpful for squaring up the corners of your quilt top.

4. Piece the red 1½" x 42" strips together end to end and cut two strips, 84½" long, and two strips, 86½" long.

5. Sew the red 84½"-long border strips to two opposite sides of the quilt center and press. Sew the 86½"-long border strips to the top and bottom of the quilt center and press. The quilt should measure 86½" square.

6. Piece the tan 2" x 42" strips together end to end and cut two strips, 86½" long, and two strips, 89½" long, for the middle border.

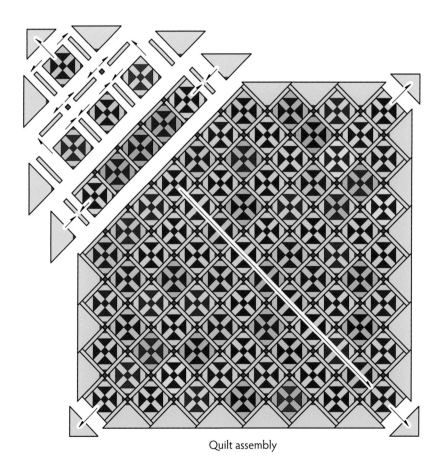

Quilt assembly

7. Sew the tan 86½"-long border strips to the sides of the quilt and press. Sew the 89½"-long border strips to the top and bottom of the quilt and press. The quilt should measure 89½" square.

8. Piece the blue 3½" x 42" strips together end to end and cut two strips, 89½" long, and two strips, 95½" long, for the outer border.

9. Sew the blue 89½"-long border strips to opposite sides of the quilt and press. Sew the 95½"-long border strips to the top and bottom of the quilt and press. The quilt top should measure 95½" square.

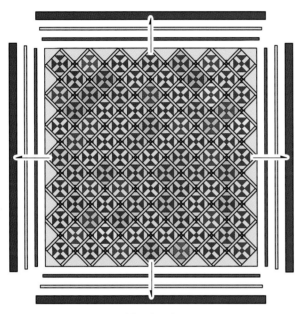

Adding borders

Finishing

Visit ShopMartingale.com/HowtoQuilt for more details on quilting and finishing.

1. Layer the backing, batting, and quilt top; baste the layers together. Hand or machine quilt as desired. Laura's quilt features machine-quilted Baptist fans.

2. Use the blue 2½"-wide strips to make the binding and attach it to the quilt.

Summer Dash by April Rosenthal
Finished quilt: 60½" x 76½" • Finished blocks: 6" x 6"

Summer Dash

A classic Churn
Dash looks extra
sweet in a scrappy mix
of sunny florals and
plaids. Framing the
blocks with sashing
and cornerstones is a
simple way to add pop
to the design.

Materials

Yardage is based on 42"-wide fabric. Fat quarters measure approximately 18" x 21".

16 assorted print fat quarters for blocks and sashing

2½ yards of white solid for blocks and border

⅔ yard of plaid for binding*

4¾ yards of fabric for backing

68" x 85" piece of batting

*April used a plaid printed on the diagonal. If you use a woven plaid, you may want to cut binding strips on the bias to get the same look.

Cutting

All measurements include ¼"-wide seam allowances. For the fat quarters, refer to the cutting diagram below to ensure you have enough fabric.

From *each* of the print fat quarters, cut:*

    8 rectangles, 2½" x 6½" (128 total)

    16 rectangles, 1½" x 2½" (256 total)

    8 squares, 3" x 3" (128 total)

    7 squares, 2½" x 2½" (112 total)

*Set aside the 2½" x 6½" rectangles and 3 of the 2½" squares from each fat quarter for the sashing.

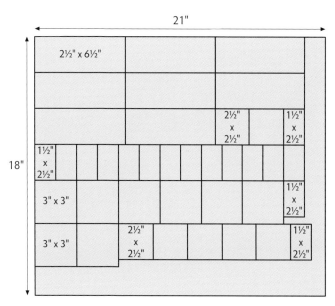

Fat-quarter cutting

Continued on page 52

Continued from page 51

From the white solid, cut:

10 strips, 2½" x 42; crosscut into 252 rectangles, 1½" x 2½"

10 strips, 3" x 42"; crosscut into 126 squares, 3" x 3"

7 strips, 3½" x 42"

From the plaid, cut:

8 strips, 2½" x 42"

Making the Churn Dash Blocks

Press all seam allowances as shown by the arrows in the illustrations.

1. Draw a diagonal line from corner to corner on the wrong side of each white 3" square. Pair each white 3" square with a print 3" square with right sides together. Stitch a scant ¼" from each side of the marked line. Cut on the marked line and press. Trim to 2½" square. Make 252 half-square-triangle units.

Make 252.

2. Pair each white 1½" x 2½" rectangle with a print 1½" x 2½" rectangle. Stitch along one long side; press. Make 252 rectangle units.

Make 252.

3. Lay out four matching half-square-triangle units, four matching rectangle units, and a matching 2½" square as shown. Sew the units into rows and press. Stitch the rows together; press. The block should measure 6½" square. Make 63 blocks. Note that you'll have a few leftover pieces, enough for one additional block.

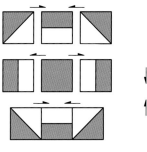 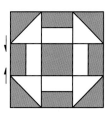

Make 63.

Assembling the Quilt

1. Lay out the blocks in nine rows of seven blocks each as shown. When you're happy with the color placement, add the 2½" x 6½" sashing rectangles so that the sashing fabric matches every other Churn Dash block. Place the assorted 2½" sashing squares randomly. You'll have extra sashing rectangles to use in another project.

2. Piece the blocks together in rows and press. Stitch the rows together, nesting the seams. Press.

3. Piece the white 3½" x 42" strips together into one long strip. Measure the width of the quilt through the center. It should measure 54½". Cut two white strips to this length and sew them to the top and bottom of the quilt. Press the seam allowances toward the border. Measure the length of the quilt through the center. It should measure 76½". Cut two white strips to this length and sew them to the sides of the quilt top. Press the seam allowances toward the borders.

Finishing

Visit ShopMartingale.com/HowtoQuilt for more details on quilting and finishing.

1. Layer the backing, batting, and quilt top; baste the layers together. Hand or machine quilt as desired. April machine quilted her quilt with an allover design of intersecting arcs.

2. Use the plaid 2½"-wide strips to make the binding and attach it to the quilt.

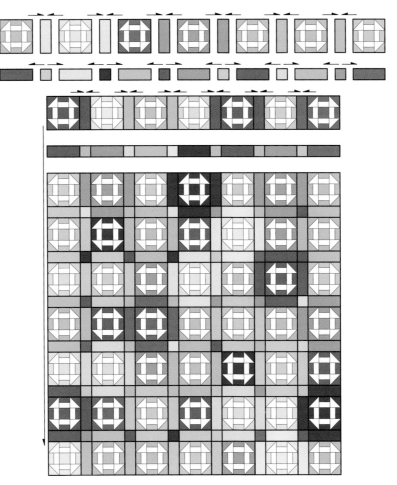

Quilt assembly

Scrap Bin Runner by Tammy Vonderschmitt

Finished runner: Approximately 19" x 42" • **Finished blocks:** 8" x 8"

Scrap Bin Runner

*P*ut a spin on the traditional Churn Dash by placing a pinwheel in the center, and then add another twist by arranging the blocks in an unconventional layout. This striking table runner consists of just eight blocks, so it's perfectly suited to using small scraps from your stash.

Materials

Yardage is based on 42"-wide fabric.

⅝ yard *total* of assorted light prints for blocks
¼ yard *total* of assorted red prints for blocks
¼ yard *total* of assorted blue prints for blocks
⅜ yard of navy tone on tone for binding
1½ yards of fabric for backing
27" x 50" piece of batting

Cutting

All measurements include ¼"-wide seam allowances. Each block requires a red or blue print for the pinwheel unit, a red or blue print for the Churn Dash, and three different light prints. Cut the pieces for one block at a time; cut a total of eight blocks.

Cutting for 1 Block

From a light print for the pinwheel, cut:
    1 square, 3¼" x 3¼"; cut into quarters diagonally

From a red or blue print for the pinwheel, cut:
    1 square, 3¼" x 3¼"; cut into quarters diagonally

From a light print for the pinwheel background, cut:
    2 squares, 2⅞" x 2⅞"; cut in half diagonally to yield 4 triangles

From a light print for the Churn Dash background, cut:
    2 squares, 3" x 3"
    4 rectangles, 1½" x 4½"

From a red or blue print for the Churn Dash, cut:
    2 squares, 3" x 3"
    4 rectangles, 1½" x 4½"

Cutting for Binding

From the navy tone on tone, cut:
    4 strips, 2½" x 42"

Assembling the Blocks

Press all seam allowances as shown by the arrows in the illustrations.

1. Sew a light 3¼" triangle to a blue (or red) 3¼" triangle along the short edges; press. Make four matching triangle units.

Make 4.

2. Sew a unit from step 1 to a light 2⅞" triangle and press. Make four units that should measure 2½" square.

Make 4.

3. Arrange the four units to make the pinwheel-unit center. Sew together and press. The unit should measure 4½" square.

4. Draw a line from corner to corner on the wrong side of the two matching light 3" squares for the Churn Dash.

5. Place the marked light squares right sides together with the two matching red (or blue) 3" squares for the Churn Dash. Sew ¼" from each side of the drawn lines. Cut along the drawn lines and press. You'll have four identical half-square-triangle units. Trim each unit to 2½" square.

2½"

2½"

Make 4.

6. Sew a red (or blue) 1½" x 4½" rectangle to a light 1½" x 4½" rectangle along one long edge; press. Make four rectangle units that measure 2½" x 4½".

Make 4.

7. Lay out the four half-square-triangle units, the four rectangle units, and the pinwheel unit in three rows as shown. Join the units in each row and press. Join the rows. Press. The block should measure 8½" x 8½".

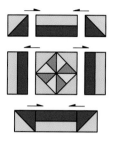 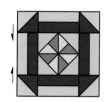

8. Repeat steps 1–7 to make a total of eight blocks with blue or red fabrics as desired. The featured quilt has five blocks with red Churn Dashes and three with blue Churn Dashes. One of the blocks has both a red pinwheel unit and a red Churn Dash. Mix and match as you like!

Assembling the Quilt Top

Arrange the blocks as shown. Join each pair of blocks in the three middle rows; press the seam allowances in one direction. Join the rows, matching the seam allowances of one row to the center of the block in the adjacent row. Press.

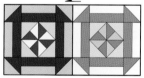

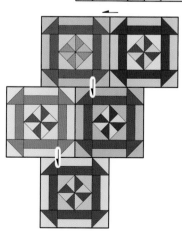

Quilt assembly

Finishing

Visit ShopMartingale.com/HowtoQuilt for more details on quilting and finishing.

1. Layer the backing, batting, and quilt top; baste the layers together. Hand or machine quilt as desired.

Tammy quilted her runner with an allover grid of straight lines spaced about ½" apart.

2. Use the navy 2½"-wide strips to make the binding and attach it to the quilt.

Binding Inside Corners

Binding inner corners can be a little tricky. Here's how Tammy does it.

1. Mark the point at each inner 90° corner where the seams will pivot.

2. Clip into the corner and grade the layers a bit to create a notch.

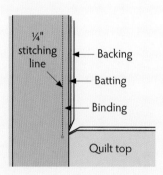

3. Stitch the binding with your usual seam allowance, but when you approach the inner point, place a pin at the corner. Stop stitching just before you reach the pin, keeping the needle down. Align the binding with the next side, remove the pin, and stitch through the point and a stitch or two beyond the point.

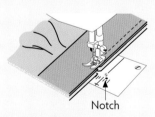

Notch

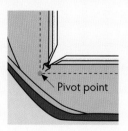

Pivot point

4. Stop stitching with the needle down and pivot the quilt to the next side and continue stitching. Continue around the quilt, repeating the process at each inner corner.

5. When hand stitching the binding to the back, fold the extra binding fabric under itself to create a miter at each inner (and outer) corner, adding a couple stitches to hold the miter in place.

Quilt back

Butterscotch and Blue by Jo Morton; quilted by Stella Schaffert

Finished quilt: 32¼" x 32¼" • **Finished blocks:** 4" x 4"

Butterscotch and Blue

Jo paired creamy butterscotch-hued fabrics with a scrappy assortment of blue prints to make a warm and welcoming small-scale Churn Dash quilt. Setting the blocks on point and adding sashing creates a lattice-like look.

Materials

Yardage is based on 42"-wide fabric.

¾ yard of blue print for outer border

¾ yard of butterscotch print A for sashing and inner border

½ yard of butterscotch print B for setting triangles and binding

13 squares, 10" x 10", of assorted blue and brown prints for blocks

13 squares, 10" x 10", of assorted tan prints for blocks

1 square, 10" x 10", of butterscotch plaid for border corner squares

1 square, 12" x 12", of dark blue print for sashing squares and inner border squares

1⅛ yards of fabric for backing

38" x 38" piece of batting

Cutting

All measurements include ¼"-wide seam allowances. Cutting is for 1 block; you'll need a total of 13 blocks.

Cutting for 1 Block

From 1 blue or brown 10" square, cut:

    2 squares, 2⅜" x 2⅜"

    1 rectangle, 1¼" x 7"

    1 square, 1½" x 1½"

From 1 tan 10" square, cut:

    2 squares, 2⅜" x 2⅜"

    1 rectangle, 1¼" x 7"

Cutting for the Remainder of the Quilt

From butterscotch print A, cut *on the lengthwise grain*:

    4 strips, 1¼" x 22¾"

From the remainder of butterscotch print A, cut *on the crosswise grain*:

    2 strips, 4½" x 36"; crosscut into 36 rectangles, 1¾" x 4½

From the dark blue print, cut:

    24 squares, 1¾" x 1¾"

    4 squares, 1¼" x 1 ¼"

Continued on page 60

Continued from page 59

From butterscotch print B, cut:

2 squares, 9" x 9"; cut into quarters diagonally to yield 8 triangles

2 squares, 5½" x 5½"; cut in half diagonally to yield 4 triangles

4 binding strips, 1⅛" x 42"

From the butterscotch plaid, cut:

4 squares, 4½" x 4½"

From the blue print, cut *on the lengthwise grain:*

4 strips, 4½" x 24¼"

Making the Churn Dash Blocks

Press all seam allowances as shown by the arrows in the illustrations.

1. Use a pencil to draw a diagonal line from corner to corner on the wrong side of the two matching tan 2⅜" squares. Layer each with a matching blue or brown 2⅜" square, right sides together. Sew ¼" from each side of the drawn lines. Cut along the pencil line. Make four half-square-triangle units that measure 2" square.

Make 4.

2. Sew the matching blue 1¼" x 7" rectangle to the matching tan 1¼" x 7" rectangle along the 7" side. Cut the strip set into four segments, 1½" wide.

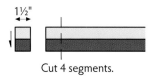

1½"

Cut 4 segments.

3. Lay out the four half-square-triangle units, the four strip-set segments, and the matching blue 1½" square as shown. Join the pieces into rows. Join the rows, and then refer to "Clipping Trick" above right to press the center of each row toward

the center of the block. Press. The block should measure 4½" square.

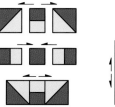

4. Repeat steps 1–3 to make 13 blocks.

Clipping Trick

At the four center seam intersections, clip into the seam allowance on each side, ¼" from the stitching (clips will be ½" apart). Press the seam allowances open between the clips.

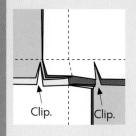 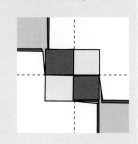

Clip. Clip.

Assembling the Quilt

1. Arrange the Churn Dash blocks on point in rows of three blocks across and three blocks down. Fill in the gaps with the remaining four Churn Dash blocks. Add the butterscotch 1¾" x 4½" sashing rectangles, dark blue 1¾" sashing squares, and butterscotch 9" and 5½" setting triangles.

2. Join the blocks, sashing, and side setting triangles in diagonal rows. Join the sashing and sashing squares in rows.

3. Pin and sew a sashing row to a block row, matching the seam intersections. Use the "Clipping Trick" on the seam intersections. Press. When all the

sashing rows and block rows are joined, add the corner triangles.

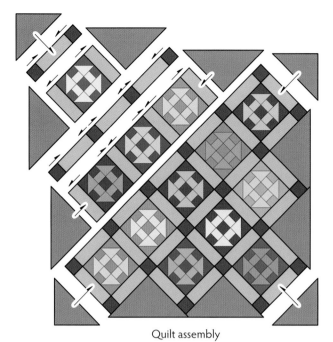

Quilt assembly

4. Trim the edges, leaving a ¼" seam allowance beyond the corners of the sashing rectangles and ¼" beyond the diagonal half of the outer sashing squares. The quilt top should now measure 22¾" x 22¾". If your dimensions are slightly different, cut the inner and outer borders to fit the dimensions of your quilt rather than those given.

Align point with ¼"
mark on ruler. Trim.

5. Pin and sew the butterscotch 1¼" x 22¾" inner-border strips to the sides of the quilt.

6. Sew the dark blue 1¼" squares to both sides of the remaining border strips and press. Pin and sew the borders to the top and bottom of the quilt, matching the seam intersections. Press. Use the "Clipping Trick" at the seam intersection. The top should now measure 24¼" x 24¼".

7. Pin and sew the blue 4½" x 24¼" border strips to the sides of the quilt.

8. Sew the plaid 4½" squares to both sides of the remaining border strips. Pin and sew these borders to the top and bottom of the quilt, matching the seam intersections. Use the "Clipping Trick" at the seam intersection and press. The top should measure 32¼" x 32¼".

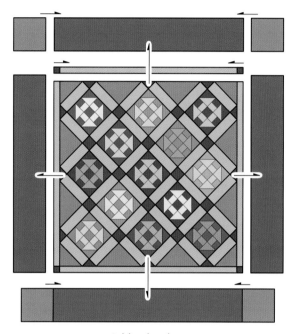

Adding borders

Finishing

Visit ShopMartingale.com/HowtoQuilt for more details on quilting and finishing.

1. Layer the backing, batting, and quilt top; baste the layers together. Hand or machine quilt as desired. Stella quilted the blocks, sashing, and inner borders in the ditch. She quilted an S curve on the sashing strips and a cable design in the outer border.

2. Use the butterscotch 1⅛"-wide strips to make the binding. Jo prefers a single-fold binding on her quilts. A double-thickness binding is too heavy for most small quilts and can contribute to a wavy edge. To attach single-fold binding, stitch the binding to the quilt top, and then fold the binding to the back, turn under ¼", and pin in place. Blind stitch or slip-stitch the binding to the back of the quilt using close, small stitches.

Little Boy Blue by Tonya Alexander; quilted by Tracey Fisher
Finished size: 48½" x 48½" • **Finished blocks:** 6" x 6", 12" x 12", 18" x 18", and 24" x 24"

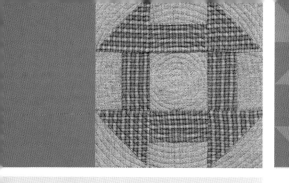

Little Boy Blue

*T*ake a modern approach to the classic Churn Dash by experimenting with the scale, size, and placement of the blocks within one quilt. A simple blue-and-gray color scheme gives the different design elements a sense of unity.

Materials

Yardage is based on 42"-wide fabric.

2⅛ yards of gray print for blocks, background, and binding

⅔ yard of navy solid for border block

⅜ yard of blue plaid for 24" block

⅛ yard *each* of blue tone on tone, navy plaid, and blue stripe for 6" blocks

¼ yard *each* of blue solid and light blue plaid for 12" blocks

¼ yard of dark blue plaid for 18" block

3⅛ yard of fabric for backing

57" x 57" piece of batting

Cutting

All measurements include ¼"-wide seam allowances.

From the gray print, cut:

1 strip, 3" x 42"; crosscut into 6 squares, 3" x 3"

2 strips, 2½" x 42"; crosscut into:
- 12 rectangles, 1½" x 2½"
- 3 squares, 2½" x 2½"
- 8 rectangles, 2½" x 4½"

1 strip, 5" x 42"; crosscut into:
- 4 squares, 5" x 5"
- 2 squares, 4½" x 4½"

2 strips, 7" x 42"; crosscut into 6 squares, 7" x 7"*

2 strips, 3½" x 42"; crosscut into:
- 4 rectangles, 3½" x 12½"
- 4 rectangles, 3½" x 6½"

1 strip, 6½" x 42"; crosscut into:
- 1 rectangle, 6½" x 12½"
- 3 squares, 6½" x 6½"

4 strips, 3½" x 36½"

6 binding strips, 2½" x 42"

From the blue tone on tone, cut:

2 squares, 3" x 3"

4 rectangles, 1½" x 2½"

*You may be able to cut the 7 squares from 1 strip.

Continued on page 64

Continued from page 63

From the navy plaid, cut:
4 squares, 3" x 3"
8 rectangles, 1½" x 2½"

From the blue stripe, cut:
4 squares, 3" x 3"
8 rectangles, 1½" x 2½"
1 square, 2½" x 2½"

From the blue solid, cut:
1 strip, 5" x 42"; crosscut into:
• 2 squares, 5" x 5"
• 4 rectangles, 2½" x 4½"

From the light blue plaid, cut:
1 strip, 5" x 42"; crosscut into:
• 2 squares, 5" x 5"
• 4 rectangles, 2½" x 4½"

From the blue plaid, cut:
1 strip, 3½" x 42"; crosscut into 3 rectangles, 3½" x 12½"
1 strip, 7" x 42"; crosscut into:
• 2 squares, 7" x 7"
• 1 rectangle, 3½" x 12½"

From the dark blue plaid, cut:
1 strip, 7" x 42"; crosscut into:
• 2 squares, 7" x 7"
• 4 rectangles, 3½" x 6½"

From the navy solid, cut:
4 strips, 3½" x 36½"
2 squares, 7" x 7"

Making the Blocks

Press all seam allowances as shown by the arrows in the illustrations.

1. Pair two gray 3" squares and two blue tone on tone 3" squares right sides together. Draw a diagonal line from corner to corner on the wrong side of the gray squares and stitch ¼" from each side of the drawn line.

2. Cut on the drawn line and press. Make four half-square-triangle units. Trim to 2½" x 2½".

Make 4.

3. Sew a gray 1½" x 2½" rectangle to a blue tone on tone 1½" x 2½" rectangle along the long edges; press. Make four matching units.

Make 4.

4. Lay out the four half-square-triangle units, the four matching units from step 3, and a gray 2½" square as shown. Join units into rows; press. Sew the rows together to make the block and press.

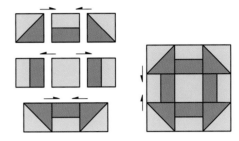

5. Repeat steps 1–4 with the navy plaid, blue stripe, and gray fabrics to make two 6½" Churn Dash blocks with gray backgrounds.

6. Repeat steps 1–4 with navy plaid and blue stripe fabrics to make one 6½" Churn Dash block with a blue stripe background.

Make 1.

7. Repeat steps 1–4 with the blue solid, light blue plaid, and gray 5" squares and 2½" x 4½" rectangles, plus the gray 4½" squares. Trim the half-square-triangle units to 4½" x 4½". Make two Churn Dash blocks that measure 12½" x 12½".

8. Repeat steps 1 and 2 with the blue plaid, dark blue plaid, and gray 7" squares to make eight half-square-triangle units. Trim to 6½" x 6½".

9. Sew a dark blue plaid and a gray 3½" x 6½" rectangle together along the long edges; press. Make four.

10. Arrange three of the dark blue plaid half-square-triangle units, one blue plaid half-square-triangle unit, the units from step 9, and the block from step 6 as shown to make a larger Churn Dash block. (You'll have one dark blue plaid and gray half-square-triangle unit left over.) Sew the units into rows and press. Sew the rows together; press. This will create the upper-left quadrant of the quilt center.

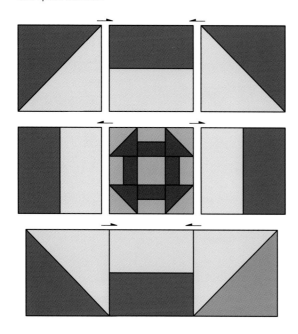

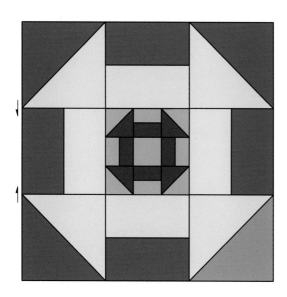

11. Sew a blue plaid and gray 3½" x 12½" rectangle together along the long edges. Press. Make four rectangle units

Make 4.

Assembling the Quilt Top

1. To assemble the upper-right quadrant of the quilt center, lay out the gray 6½" x 12½" rectangle, one 12½" Churn Dash block, one 6½" half-square-triangle unit from step 8 of "Making the Blocks," and one gray/blue 6½" x 12½" rectangle unit from step 11 as shown. Sew the rectangle to the block and press. Sew the lower units together, press, and join them to the block section.

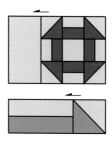
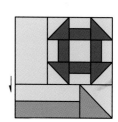

2. For the lower-left quadrant, lay out the three 6½" Churn Dash blocks, three 6½" gray squares, one blue plaid 6½" half-square-triangle unit from step 8, and one gray/blue plaid 6½" x 12½" rectangle unit from step 11 as shown. Sew the blocks and units into three vertical rows and press as shown. Sew the rows together and press.

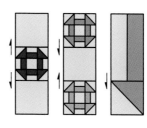
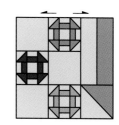

3. For the lower-right quadrant, lay out the remaining 12½" Churn Dash block, one blue plaid 6½" half-square-triangle unit from step 8, and two gray/blue plaid 6½" x 12½" rectangle units from step 11 as shown. Sew the block to a rectangle unit and press. Sew the rectangle unit and half-square-triangle unit together and press. Sew the two sections together; press.

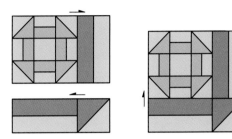

4. Sew the upper-left and upper-right quadrants together and press. Sew the lower-left and lower-right quadrants together and press. Join the two halves to complete the center. Press.

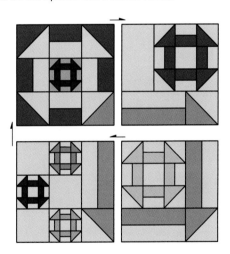

5. Sew navy solid and gray 3½" x 36½" strips together to make a border. Press the seam allowances toward the navy. Make four borders.

Make 4.

6. Sew border strips to the left and right sides of the quilt center, making sure that the gray is along the outside edge. Press.

7. Make four half-square-triangle units using two navy and the remaining two gray 7" squares. Trim the half-square-triangle units to 6½" x 6½".

8. Sew a half-square-triangle unit to each end of the remaining border units and press. Sew to the top and bottom of the quilt and press.

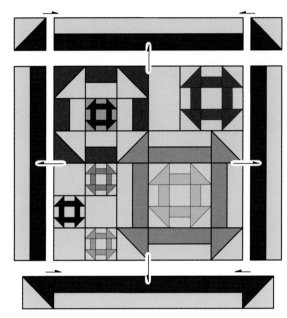

Quilt assembly

Finishing

Visit ShopMartingale.com/HowtoQuilt for more details on quilting and finishing.

1. Layer the backing, batting, and quilt top; baste the layers together. Hand or machine quilt as desired. Tracey quilted this project with echoing circles of varying sizes across the surface of the quilt.

2. Trim the corners to approximately 1" beyond the seam line of the half-square-triangle units.

3. Use the gray 2½"-wide strips to make the binding and attach it to the quilt.

Dreaming in Color

*D*elve into your stash to make an eclectic rainbow of Churn Dash blocks. Use bright prints for the blocks and light or low-volume prints for the background—the scrappier the better!

Materials

Yardage is based on 42"-wide fabric.

2⅓ yards *total* of assorted light scraps for blocks
1⅔ yards *total* of assorted dark scraps for blocks
2 yards of large-scale floral for outer border
⅞ yard of green print for inner border and binding
4 yards of fabric for backing
70" x 76" piece of batting

Cutting

All measurements include ¼"-wide seam allowances.

From the assorted light scraps, cut:
    224 squares, 2¾" x 2¾"
    224 rectangles, 2" x 2¾"

From the assorted dark scraps, cut:
    56 *sets of 4* matching squares, 2" x 2" (224 total)
    56 *sets of 4* matching rectangles, 1¼" x 2¾" (224 total)
    56 squares, 2¾" x 2¾"

From the green print, cut:
    6 strips, 1½" x 42"
    7 binding strips, 2½" x 42"

From the large-scale floral, cut *on the lengthwise grain:*
    2 strips, 6½" x 56½"
    2 strips, 6½" x 61¾"

Assembling the Blocks

Press all seam allowances as shown by the arrows in the illustrations.

1. Sew four matching dark 1¼" x 2¾" rectangles to four light 2" x 2¾" rectangles. Press. Make four units for one block.

Make 4.

2. Select four matching dark 2" squares and four light 2¾" squares. Using a ruler and a mechanical pencil, draw a diagonal line from corner to corner on the wrong sides of the 2" squares.

Dreaming in Color by Kim Brackett

Finished quilt: 61¾" x 68½" • **Finished blocks:** 6¾" x 6¾"

3. Place a marked square on top of a light 2¾" square, right sides together and corners aligned. Sew on the drawn line. Fold up the square and match the corners and edges to make sure you've sewn accurately, adjusting the seam allowance if needed. Then press the triangle in place. Fold the triangle back down and trim the excess fabric, leaving ¼" seam allowances. Press back into place. Make four units for one block.

Make 4.

4. Arrange the four units from step 3, the four units from step 1, and a dark 2¾" square as shown. Sew the units into rows and press. Sew the rows together and press to complete the block. The block should measure 7¼" square.

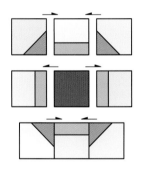 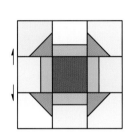

5. Repeat steps 1–4 to make a total of 56 blocks.

Assembling the Quilt

1. Arrange the blocks in eight horizontal rows of seven blocks each as shown at right. Sew the

blocks into rows and press. Sew the rows together and press.

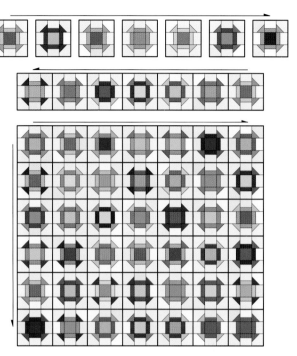

Quilt assembly

2. Sew the green 1½" x 42" strips together end to end to make one long strip. Cut two strips, 54½" long, and two strips, 49¾" long. Sew the longer strips to the sides of the quilt and press the seam allowances toward the green borders. Sew the shorter strips to the top and bottom of the quilt and press.

3. Sew the floral strips together end to end to make one long strip. Cut two strips 56½" long and two strips 61¾" long. Sew the longer strips to the sides of the quilt and press the seam allowances toward the floral borders. Sew the shorter strips to the top and bottom of the quilt and press.

Finishing

Visit ShopMartingale.com/HowtoQuilt for more details on quilting and finishing.

1. Layer the backing, batting, and quilt top; baste the layers together. Hand or machine quilt as desired. Kim's quilt was quilted with an allover design of flowers, leaves, swirls, and curling tendrils.

2. Use the green 2½"-wide strips to make the binding and attach it to the quilt.

Wavy Churn by Gina Reddin; quilted by Michelle Banton
Finished quilt: 56" x 70"

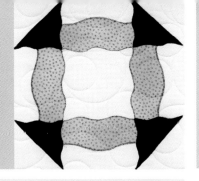

Wavy Churn

*S*kip the piecing altogether by making a quilt adorned with appliquéd Churn Dashes. The bright colors and curvy edges add another fun departure from the traditional design.

Materials

Yardage is based on 42"-wide fabric. Fat quarters measure approximately 18" x 21" and fat eighths measure approximately 9" x 21".

3⅓ yards of white solid for background

6 assorted bright fat eighths for appliqué

1 dark fat quarter for appliqué

⅝ yard of black solid for binding

3⅝ yards of fabric for backing

64" x 78" piece of batting

2 yards of 18"-wide, lightweight fusible web (such as Lite Steam-A-Seam 2)

Air or water-soluble marking pen

Cutting

All measurements include ¼"-wide seam allowances.

From the white solid, cut:

2 pieces, 42" x 60"

From the black solid, cut:

7 strips, 2½" x 42"

Preparing the Appliqués

1. Trace the appliqué patterns on page 74 onto the paper side of the fusible web. Trace 12 of the Churn Dash shapes and 48 of the corner shapes. Cut around the shapes, leaving approximately ¼" of space beyond the lines.

Cutting Trick

To more easily cut out the center of the Churn Dash, you can cut through a corner as shown by the dashed line, and then cut along the inside line. The cut will be covered by one of the black corner pieces. As for the inner piece you're cutting away, save it to use in future projects.

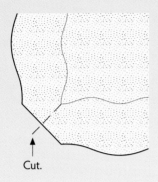

Cut.

2. Fuse the 48 corner shapes to the wrong side of the dark fat quarter, following the manufacturer's instructions. Fuse two Churn Dash shapes to the wrong side of each of the bright fat eighths. Allow to cool; then use scissors to cut out the appliqué pieces along the traced lines. Remove the paper backing from all the appliqué pieces.

Appliquéing the Quilt Top

1. Sew the two white background pieces together along the 60" length. Press the seam allowances open. Trim to make a background rectangle measuring 56" x 70".

2. Referring to the placement guide on page 73, measure and use an air- or water-soluble marker to mark the background fabric for positioning the appliqués. Begin marking in the lower-right corner. Measure up 4½" and over 8¾" to make the first dot. Measure 4" to the left of that and mark a second dot. The dots will be used to line up the inner corners of the larger Churn Dash piece. Allow 4" across from corner to corner for each Churn Dash.

3. Continue to mark the placement of the remaining five Churn Dashes in the lower-right corner, referring to the placement guide.

4. Repeat the process to mark the upper-left corner.

5. Arrange the large appliqués on the background as shown on page 73, matching the inside upper or lower corners of each appliqué to the dots on the background fabric. The dots should be covered just slightly by the appliqués. Press with your hand to ensure that the appliqués are flat and that any cut corners butt up next to each other. Follow the manufacturer's instructions to fuse in place.

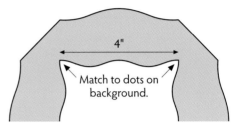

4"

Match to dots on background.

6. Place a dark corner appliqué over the straight edges of each Churn Dash piece, matching the outer point of the corner to the inner point of the Churn Dash. Fuse in place.

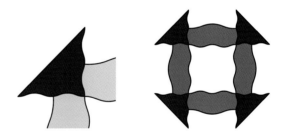

7. Set your machine for a small zigzag (Gina used a 2.5 mm width and 1 mm length). You can also stitch the edges with a machine blanket stitch or other decorative stitch. Sew around all edges of the appliqués to secure them.

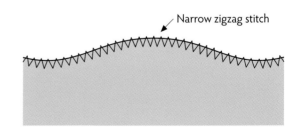

Narrow zigzag stitch

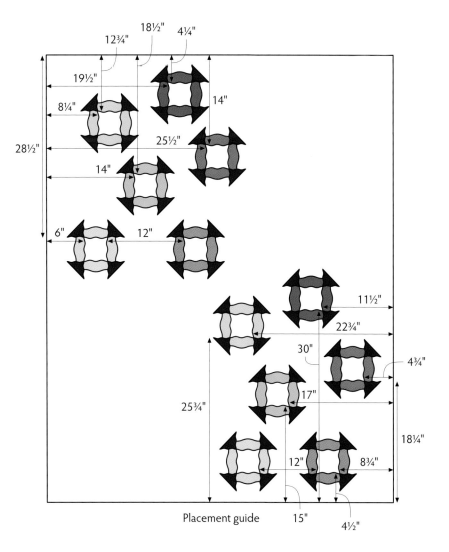

Placement guide

Finishing

Visit ShopMartingale.com/HowtoQuilt for more details on quilting and finishing.

1. Layer the backing, batting, and quilt top; baste the layers together. Hand or machine quilt as desired. Gina's quilt was quilted with an allover design of loops and circles.

2. Use the black 2½"-wide strips to make the binding and attach it to the quilt.

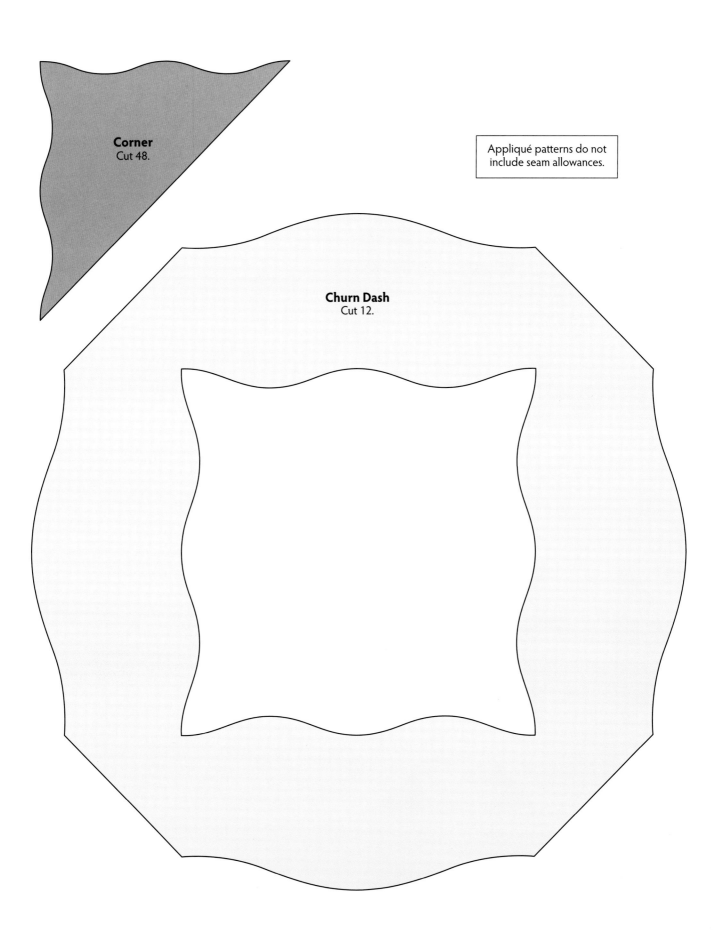

Corner
Cut 48.

Appliqué patterns do not
include seam allowances.

Churn Dash
Cut 12.

Sweet Cream

*K*imberly chose a springy selection of aqua, green, and coral prints to make nine cheerful Double Churn Dash blocks. The simple grid layout gives the quilt a fresh, graphic look.

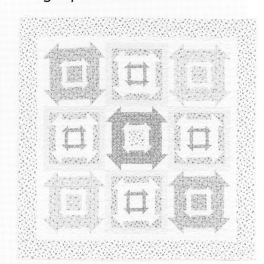

Materials

Yardage is based on 42"-wide fabric.

⅞ yard of white solid for blocks and inner border
⅔ yard of aqua print A for blocks and binding
½ yard of cream floral for center block and border
⅓ yard *each* of aqua print B and green print for blocks
¼ yard of coral print for blocks
¼ yard of gray floral for blocks
2½ yards of fabric for backing
44" x 44" piece of batting

Cutting

All measurements include ¼"-wide seam allowances.

From the white solid, cut:

1 strip, 3⅜" x 42"; crosscut into 10 squares, 3⅜" x 3⅜"
1 strip, 2⅞" x 42"; crosscut into:
- 8 squares, 2⅞" x 2⅞"
- 4 squares, 2½" x 2½"

1 strip, 2⅛" x 42"; crosscut into:
- 10 squares, 2⅛" x 2⅛"
- 8 squares, 1⅞" x 1⅞"

9 strips, 1½" x 42"; crosscut into:
- 20 rectangles, 1½" x 5½"
- 16 rectangles, 1½" x 4½"
- 2 strips, 1½" x 30½"
- 2 strips, 1½" x 32½"

1 strip, 3" x 42"; crosscut into:
- 20 rectangles, 1¼" x 3"
- 16 rectangles, 1" x 2½"

From *each* of the green print and aqua print B, cut:

4 squares, 3⅜" x 3⅜" (8 total)
4 squares, 2⅛" x 2⅛" (8 total)
8 rectangles, 2" x 5½" (16 total)
8 rectangles, 1" x 3" (16 total)
2 squares, 3" x 3" (4 total)

Continued on page 77

Sweet Cream by Kimberly Jolly

Finished quilt: 38½" x 38½" • **Finished blocks:** 10" x 10"

Continued from page 75

From the coral print, cut:

2 squares, 3⅜" x 3⅜"

2 squares, 2⅛" x 2⅛"

4 rectangles, 2" x 5½"

8 squares, 1⅞" x 1⅞"

4 rectangles, 1" x 3"

16 rectangles, 1" x 2½"

From the gray floral, cut:

1 strip, 2⅞" x 42"; crosscut into

8 squares, 2⅞" x 2⅞"

2 strips, 1½" x 42"; crosscut into

16 rectangles, 1½" x 4½"

From the cream floral, cut:

2 strips, 3½" x 38½"

2 strips, 3½" x 32½"

1 square, 3" x 3"

From aqua print A, cut:

5 strips, 1½" x 42"; crosscut into:

• 8 strips, 1½" x 10½"

• 8 strips, 1½" x 8½"

5 binding strips, 2½" x 42"

Assembling the A Blocks

You'll make two green A blocks, two aqua A blocks, and one coral A block. Press all seam allowances as shown by the arrows in the illustrations.

1. Draw a line from corner to corner on the wrong side of the white 2⅛" squares. Place a marked square right sides together with a green 2⅛" square. Sew ¼" from each side of the drawn line. Cut along the drawn line and press to yield two half-square-triangle units. The unit should measure 1¾" square. Make eight green/white half-square-triangle units.

Make 8.

2. Repeat step 1 with four white 3⅜" squares and four green 3⅜" squares to make eight green/white half-square-triangle units that measure 3" square.

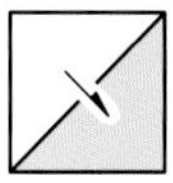

Make 8.

3. Sew a white 1¼" x 3" rectangle to a green 1" x 3" rectangle along the long edges and press. Make eight green/white rectangle units.

Make 8.

4. Repeat step 3 with eight white 1½" x 5½" rectangles and eight green 2" x 5½" rectangles to make eight green/white rectangle units.

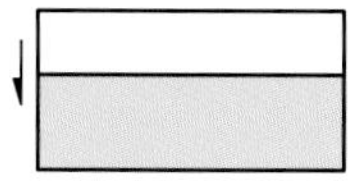

Make 8.

5. Lay out four green/white 1¾" half-square-triangle units, four green/white 3" rectangle units, and one green 3" square in three rows as shown. Join the units in each row and press. Join the rows; press. Make two green/white block centers.

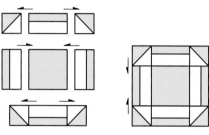

Make 2.

6. Lay out four green/white 3" half-square-triangle units, four green/white 5½" rectangle units, and one block center in three rows as shown. Join the units in each row; press. Join the rows and press. The blocks should measure 10½" square. Make two green A Blocks.

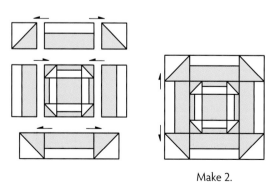

Make 2.

7. Repeat steps 1–6 to make two aqua A blocks and one coral A block. For the coral block, use the cream floral 3" square in the center.

Assembling the B Blocks

The four B blocks are identical, made from the white solid, the coral print, the gray floral, and aqua print A.

1. Make 16 coral/white half-square-triangle units using the 1⅞" squares of white and coral. The units should measure 1½" square. Make 16 gray/white half-square-triangle units using the 2⅞" squares of gray floral and white. The units should measure 2½" square.

Make 16. Make 16.

2. Make 16 coral/white rectangle units using the 1" x 2½" rectangles of white and coral. Make 16 gray/white rectangle units using the 1½" x 4½" rectangles of gray and white.

Make 16.

Make 16.

3. Lay out four coral/white half-square-triangle units, four coral/white rectangle units, and a white 2½" square as shown. Join the units into rows and then join the rows; press. Make four.

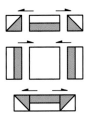

Make 4.

4. Add the gray/white rectangle units and half-square-triangle units to the block unit. Make four block centers.

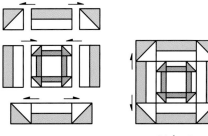

Make 4.

5. Sew the 1½" x 8½" aqua #1 strips to the sides of the block center. Press the seam allowances toward the strips. Sew the 1½" x 10½" aqua A strips to the top and bottom; press. The blocks should measure 10½" square. Make four B blocks.

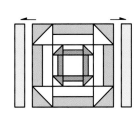 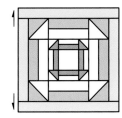

Make 4.

Assembling the Quilt

1. Lay out the blocks in three rows of three as shown in the quilt assembly diagram below. Join the blocks in each row and press. Join the rows; press. The quilt center should measure 30½" square.

2. Sew the white 1½" x 30½" strips to the sides of the quilt center. Press. Sew the white 1½" x 32½" strips to the top and bottom of the quilt center and press.

3. Sew the floral 3½" x 32½" strips to the sides of the quilt and press. Sew the floral 3½" x 38½" strips to the top and bottom; press.

Finishing the Quilt

Visit ShopMartingale.com/HowtoQuilt for more details on quilting and finishing.

1. Layer the backing, batting, and quilt top; baste the layers together. Hand or machine quilt as desired. Kimberly's quilt is machine quilted in an allover floral/swirl design.

2. Use the 2½"-wide aqua A strips to make the binding and attach it to the quilt.

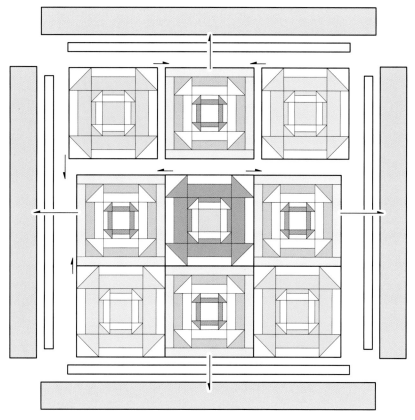

Quilt assembly

About the Contributors

Tonya Alexander

Tonya says that she's an accidental quilter by home-decorating necessity; her first quilt was meant to be her only quilt. But a love of fabric quickly overtook her. She is the author of *Stash Lab* (Martingale, 2015). Visit Tonya at EyeCandyQuilts.blogspot.com.

Laura Boehnke

A quilter and pattern designer, Laura Boehnke tests patterns for *American Patchwork and Quilting* magazine.

Kim Brackett

Kim Brackett developed an interest in quilting in 1988 after admiring a collection of vintage quilts displayed in an antique shop. She began gathering tools, fabrics, and patterns and finally finished her first quilt 10 years later. Since then she has completed countless quilts, many of which have been featured in her books. Visit her at MagnoliaBayQuilts.blogspot.com

Kari M. Carr

A proud member of the Creative Grids Ruler design team and a BERNINA ambassador, Kari is the owner of New Leaf Stitches, a pattern-design company, and creator of the innovative notion Clearly Perfect Angles. You can find Kari at NewLeafStitches.com.

Kim Diehl

With just the third quilt she'd ever made, self-taught quiltmaker Kim Diehl became the winner of *American Patchwork and Quilting* magazine's "Pieces of the Past" quilt challenge in 1998, turning her life onto a new and unexpected path. In addition to her best-selling "Simple" series of quilting books published with Martingale, Kim has designed several fabric collections for Henry Glass & Co.

Amy Ellis

Amy was amazed to discover the great source of inspiration and knowledge that makes up the blogging world, and decided to participate via Amy's Creative Side. Amy is the author of five books and contributor to many more. Visit her at AmysCreativeSide.com.

Kate Henderson

Kate Henderson learned to sew clothes at the age of 12 and has sewn for herself ever since. After her twins were born in 2005, she began designing soft toys for them and soon began selling patterns. Kate lives in the southwest of Western Australia with her husband and four girls. Visit her at NeverEnoughHours.blogspot.com.

Carol Hopkins

As a professor of literacy and language education at Purdue University, Carol Hopkins prepares future elementary teachers to teach struggling readers. Through her pattern business, she markets quilt patterns that she has designed for eighteenth- and nineteenth-century reproduction fabrics. Visit her at CarolHopkinsDesigns.com.

Kimberly Jolly

Kimberly is the owner of Fat Quarter Shop, an online fabric store, and It's Sew Emma, a pattern company. Her designs are often inspired by vintage quilts, but she can find creative seeds wherever she goes.

Jo Morton

Jo Morton's use of color and design, as well as her fine stitchery, give her quilts the feeling of being made in the nineteenth century. Jo is well known for her "Jo's Little Women Club" patterns and is the author of *Jo's Little Favorites* (Martingale, 2016). Visit Jo at JoMortonquilts.com.

Gina Reddin

Gina made many of her five children's clothes when they were young, began making quilts, and soon after discovered machine embroidery. With a degree in interior design and a background as a draftsperson, she marries her loves of computers, quilting, machine embroidery, and fabric to bring a wide array of genres into her designs.

April Rosenthal

April is a fabric designer for Moda Fabrics and an author. She's also a quilter, homemaker, wife, and mama. She loves color, making things with her hands, learning, and the wind in the trees. Visit her at AprilRosenthal.com.

Tammy Vonderschmitt

Wanting more time to spend with her children, Tammy quit her engineering job and bought a quilt shop. While she'd always sewn, she'd never made a quilt. So she hired a teacher and took her first quilt class along with her customers. Tammy had her shop, Needle in the Haystack, for 11 years and now works in marketing for Moda Fabrics.

Christa Watson

An award-winning sit-down machine quilter, Christa Watson designs quilt patterns, teaches workshops, and is the author of two machine-quilting books. Christa enjoys being a wife to her husband and a mom to her three kids. You can find her at ChristaQuilts.com.

Jackie White

A quilt teacher, lecturer, and pattern designer, Jackie has a passion for creating three-dimensional art quilts. She loves embellishing so much that half her studio is devoted to embellishments. You can find her on Facebook at Jackie's Art Quilts.